P9-CRI-762

"LEWIS GRIZZARD HAS A WAY WITH WORDS, but it is more than that. He sees and says things that most of us only dimly perceive and then don't even mention."

—*The Miami Herald*

"A heartfelt look at unconditional love."

—*The Philadelphia Inquirer*

From Atlanta's Superstar Columnist and
Best-selling Author

LEWIS GRIZZARD

My Daddy Was a Pistol
and I'm a Son of a Gun

"Funny and sometimes gut-wrenching . . . you don't even have to like Grizzard or his opinions to appreciate *My Daddy Was a Pistol*. You just need a father you love."

—*Salisbury Post* (North Carolina)

"Warmth and surprising depth . . . his daddy would be deeply pleased and proud of his son."

—*Sacramento Bee*

"Offers a stronger, sadder theme to the usual mix of good-ol'-boy joke telling. . . . By the end of the book it is hard to remember when it stopped trying to be funny and hard to forget that powerful image of a good man gone astray."

—*Kirkus Reviews*

"A bittersweet account of a son coming to grips with a broken home. . . . The younger Grizzard's brand of humor is good-ol'-boy, deeply drawlin', and occasionally red-necked. He takes no prisoners."

—*Chicago Tribune*

"A sad book, a funny book, a very human book—and one that Lewis Grizzard had to write."

—*The Courier-Times*

"His most serious book—both sad and moving."

—*Florida Times-Union*

"LEWIS GRIZZARD CAN MAKE YOU LAUGH FROM THE BELLY and a moment later you will suddenly get misty and you are certain that something has got in your eye."

—*The San Diego Union*

"LEWIS GRIZZARD IS FUNNY. Almost always. But he also has the ability to start you laughing and, while you are in the middle of a good belly laugh, change directions on you. . . . He can leave you openmouthed and with a tear in your heart."

—*The Chattanooga Times*

ALSO BY LEWIS GRIZZARD

QUANTITY SALES

Most Dell books are available at special quantity discounts when purchased in bulk by corporations, organizations, and special-interest groups. Custom imprinting or excerpting can also be done to fit special needs. For details write: Dell Publishing, 666 Fifth Avenue, New York, NY 10103. Attn.: Special Sales Department.

INDIVIDUAL SALES

Are there any Dell books you want but cannot find in your local stores? If so, you can order them directly from us. You can get any Dell book in print. Simply include the book's title, author, and ISBN number if you have it, along with a check or money order (no cash can be accepted) for the full retail price plus $1.50 to cover shipping and handling. Mail to: Dell Readers Service, P.O. Box 5057, Des Plaines, IL 60017.

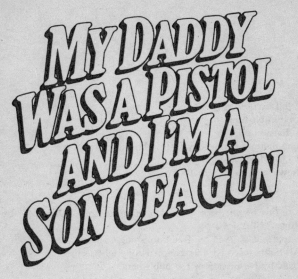

MY DADDY WAS A PISTOL AND I'M A SON OF A GUN

LEWIS GRIZZARD

A DELL BOOK

Published by
Dell Publishing
a division of
The Bantam Doubleday Dell Publishing Group, Inc.
1 Dag Hammarskjold Plaza
New York, New York 10017

The title of this book was taken from the song "Dang Me" by
Roger Miller.

For information address: Villard Books, a division of Random
House, Inc., New York, New York.

Dell ® TM 681510, Dell Publishing, a division of the Bantam
Doubleday Dell Publishing Group, Inc.

ISBN: 0-440-20006-7

Reprinted by arrangement with Villard Books, a division of
Random House, Inc.

Printed in the United States of America

June 1988

10 9 8 7 6 5 4 3 2 1

KRI

To Jim Minter, a great American,
whom I love

MY DADDY WAS A PISTOL AND I'M A SON OF A GUN

CHAPTER
1

I CANNOT DRINK AND TALK ABOUT MY FATHER, WHO DIED IN 1970, or I will cry. Sometimes, I am able to keep it to a few sniffles, but more often than not, I begin to sob when I attempt to drink and discuss my daddy. That's what I called him. Daddy.

There are various stages of intoxication of the male, of course. These have been put down by someone more clever than I, Dan Jenkins, and so I do not claim the following, but I do find it to be amusing, as well as on target:

THE TEN STAGES OF INTOXICATION
Dan Jenkins

1. WITTY AND CHARMING: This is after one or two drinks. The tongue is loosened and can yet remain in step with the brain. In the *witty and charming* state, one is likely to use foreign idioms and phrases such

as *au contraire* in place of "No way, José" or "Bull-sheyet."

2. RICH AND POWERFUL: By the third drink, you begin mentioning the little 380 SL you've had your eye on down at the Mercedes place.

3. BENEVOLENT: You'll buy her a Mercedes, too. It's only money.

4. JUST ONE MORE AND THEN WE'LL EAT: Stall tactic.

5. TO HELL WITH DINNER: Just one more and then we'll eat.

6. PATRIOTIC: The war stories begin.

7. CRANK UP THE *ENOLA GAY:* "We could have won in Nam, but . . ."

8. INVISIBLE: So this is what a Ladies' Room looks like.

9. WITTY AND CHARMING PART II: You know, you don't sweat much for a fat girl.

10. BULLETPROOF: Bull-sheyet, gimme them keys, I can drive.

I find only one thing wrong with this listing. It is incomplete. There remains one other stage, and it is a stage that I personally discovered. I likely reach it more often than most other men, but given enough to drink and the right setting, most men will arrive at this same level. I call it "CRYIN'-ABOUT-YOUR-DADDY DRUNK." I am not certain where it fits in the aforementioned list. I would guess it would fall somewhere between "7. CRANK UP THE *ENOLA GAY*" and "8. INVISIBLE," but that is only a guess and some may reach the level earlier while others reach it later. You don't need to be able to make a lot of sense when you are CAYDD, nor is it necessary to be able to make sounds intelligible to other forms of life.

I first realized this stage of intoxication some years ago after I had played tennis with a friend at his private court. If you play tennis, it always is nice, as well as convenient, to have a friend who has a private court.

We had gone three hard sets and then settled into a few late-in-the-evening cold beers, which my friend's wife dutifully delivered to the court from the refrigerator back up at the house.

"You've got a great wife," I said to my friend.

"You've just got to make them learn to appreciate you," he replied. "Other night, we were having dinner and this good-looking honey walked over and kissed me.

"My wife said, 'Who was that?'

"I said, 'That's my mistress.'

"She said, 'You've got a mistress?'

"I said, 'Sure.'

"She said, 'I'm getting a divorce.'

"I said, 'Fine, but just remember if you do, you're not going to have me around anymore to give you the things I give you. You'll have just one car, and we'll probably have to get rid of the place at the beach, and I won't be around to pay your credit card bills, either.'

"About that time, a friend of ours walked by with another young honey. My wife said, 'Who's that with Bill?'

"I said, 'That's his mistress.'

"She said, 'Ours is a lot better looking than his, isn't she?' "

We laughed together and then his wife showed up with another couple of cold beers and also a cassette player and a Willie Nelson tape. I think it was during Willie's spirited rendition of the old hymn "Precious Memories" that my friend started talking about his father. The beer . . . Willie . . . it was only a matter of time.

"I remember when my daddy died," my friend began. "We were all in the hospital room with him. The doctors had told us he wouldn't last much longer. He had emphysema and God knows what else. He opened his eyes for a moment and asked me to come close to him.

"I didn't know what he was going to say, but I knew I would be listening to his final words. I leaned over the bed so I could hear him.

" 'Son,' he said to me, 'why didn't you and your mama tell me I was going to die?'

"I said, 'Why would you ask something like that, Daddy?'

" 'Because,' he said, wheezing all the time, 'if I had known I was going to die anyway, I never would have given up smoking.' "

My friend was on a roll. He took another pull on his beer and was off on another remembrance.

"My daddy knew everybody in Atlanta, and he was always working on some deal. He ran for every political office in town. He never won anything, but it really didn't matter to him. He just enjoyed hanging around the courthouse and seeing his political ads in the paper.

"Anything he needed done or you needed done— if you were his friend—he knew a guy here or a guy there who could help. I'll never forget at his funeral, my ex-wife came over after the services to talk to my mother.

"My ex-wife got a bad case of religion after we divorced. She became one of those born-againers, and I found out she was sending about half of my alimony check to Oral Roberts every month.

"Anyway, she goes up to my mother and says, 'Margaret, you know Paw-Paw'—that's what the kids called my dad—'isn't going to heaven, don't you?'

"Mother said, 'Why not?'

"My ex-wife said, 'Because he didn't accept Jesus as his personal Savior before he died.'

"My mother thought a minute and said, 'Well, he may not get into heaven at first, but he'll meet somebody who can get him in, eventually.'"

Willie sang on, as we laughed together:

> *Preeeeecious mem-ries*
> *How they linger. . . ."*

A few moments later, I countered with a story about another friend's father.

"His daddy was really old, somewhere in his eighties or nineties, and the family was called into the hospital for his final hours.

"The old man was barely alive, and everyone in the room was a little uncomfortable. One by one, they drifted out to the hallway so they could talk and smoke, and my friend found himself alone with his father.

"His daddy had been a thrifty old coot all his life, and my buddy figured his father would like to hear about the deal he had just made at the bank. It had been a big financial story. Several banks in Atlanta were competing for money market accounts and all of them were offering an incredible twenty-five percent interest for the first month if customers would open a money market account.

"My friend leaned over his father and said, 'Daddy, you would have been real proud of me this week. I opened up a money market account at the bank that's going to pay me twenty-five percent interest a year.'

"The old man didn't respond at first and my friend thought he hadn't heard him, so he said it again: 'Daddy, you would have been real proud of me this week. I opened a money market account at the bank that's going to pay me twenty-five percent a year.'

"The old man slowly opened his eyes and looked into his son's and said, 'It's only for a month, you damn fool,' and then drifted back on out."

Cold beer goes down so easily after you've been playing tennis and perspiring a great deal. I suppose we'd had five or six each when I started talking about my own father. Daddy. I talked about the day he died.

He was living in this little town down near Savannah. He'd had a stroke on the street and after he was in the hospital a few days he got pneumonia. I was living in Atlanta and I'd been down to see him about three days earlier. He was unconscious then and was having these awful convulsions. I don't think he knew I was there.

I finally had to leave him and come back home to work. But one morning I get this phone call at about four and a nurse at the hospital tells me things are pretty bad and if I want to see him one more time while he's alive, I'd better come in a hurry.

It was over a four-hour drive down there, but I made it a lot faster. I kept praying the whole time I was driving that this whole thing was some kind of nightmare and I'd wake up.

I got to the hospital and they showed me where his room was. There were three other men in the room, men from his church. Daddy loved going to church. It's how he made friends. He would go into a church in some little town where he was going to live for a while and he'd sit right down front so everybody could see him.

He had a beautiful baritone voice, and when the singing would start, he would belt it out as loudly and as forcefully as he could. After the services, everyone would want to meet the handsome, gray-haired man with the beautiful voice.

I shook hands with the three men after I walked into the room.

"I believe your daddy's about to pass, son," one of the men said.

I looked down at him on the bed. He was a big, stout man. He'd been through two wars and all sorts of other hells, and he looked pitiful lying there in that bed. And he was blue. I swear to God he was blue.

I took his right hand. It was cold. I pressed it tightly with my hands. He didn't respond. He was breathing so slowly. One breath, and then when you didn't think he would breathe again, he would gasp for one more.

I had never seen anybody die before. I didn't know what in hell to expect. I imagined there would be doctors and nurses all around a dying man, trying to save him. There weren't. There wasn't anybody but me and three men from the church.

I asked had a doctor been in. One of the men said his doctor had come by a little earlier, but said there wasn't anything he or anybody else could do.

I really didn't know how I was supposed to act. I was twenty-three, I guess, old enough not to want to carry on in front of a roomful of other men. So I didn't cry. I even thought that maybe his dying wasn't that awful a thing. When one of his brothers, my uncle, heard he was in bad shape, he'd even thought the same thing. "He's been through enough hell as it is," is what my uncle said.

God, how I had to agree with that. There were the two wars, and when he came home from Korea, he was totally messed up. Couldn't sleep. Couldn't stay off the phone. He'd get so drunk and then get on the phone. He'd cry. Lord, he'd cry. I remember my mama fighting with him over the big telephone bills.

He started borrowing money, too. Lots of it. And nobody could figure out why. Mother would say, "Lewis, where is all that money going?"

He'd never tell her. He would never tell anybody. There was this dark secret or something. Like maybe he had done something awful and somebody was blackmailing him.

Then he skipped out on the army and started roaming. This job, that job, and you could count on a bender every now and then. Mostly now. I never knew where he was half the time. When I was a kid he let me down a lot. He'd promise, and then he wouldn't deliver. Promise he was going to straighten out and come back to me and my mother. Promise he'd take me to ball games, promise we'd go on long trips together. He'd promise me the world.

But then he wouldn't show and I wouldn't hear from him for a long time and then I'd get a money order. I suppose his conscience would get to him and he'd night wire the money, trying to make everything all right.

I never really got mad at him for those things. My mother would get mad that he would do me the way he would do me, but, somehow, I always understood. I'd be disappointed as hell, of course, but I always sensed he was doing the best he could. I really believe that when he promised me something, he had all the intentions in the world of carrying it out.

He embarrassed me a few times after I was older. I was married, and he'd show up at my house. Drunk. My wife didn't like that. He had very little family, and he started leaning on me a lot. Started asking me for money. I always gave it to him. My wife didn't like that, either.

I was still holding his hand when he took his last breath. He breathed and then he didn't breathe again. It seemed like a peaceful death. I don't think he was in any pain. I wanted to talk to him, to tell him how much I loved him, but it was better he go that way.

One of the men from the church went and got a nurse. She felt for a pulse but didn't find one. Without a word, she went out of the room, then came back with a doctor. The doctor put his stethoscope on Daddy's chest and listened. I was still holding his hand, when the doctor looked at me and said, "He's gone."

I let go of his hand. The nurse pulled the sheet over his head and then went out of the room behind the doctor. One of the three men said we ought to pray, and so he said a prayer. I don't remember which one, though.

I was in a daze.

I called my mother. She said she was sorry. I knew she was, both for me and for her. My daddy was not the kind of man you could stop loving, no matter what he did to you.

Then I called my uncle and he said he'd make some arrangements about bringing the body back to Atlanta, about the funeral. After I hung up, I had no idea what to do next.

There was the hospital bill. It was eight hundred dollars. Daddy didn't have any insurance. I didn't have eight hundred dollars. A good friend helped me pay it. They had said they wouldn't let the body go until I paid the bill. A woman said it was hospital policy to get this sort of thing cleared up as quickly as possible.

All Daddy had was in one of those plastic garbage bags. I remember opening the bag and going through his belongings. There were the clothes he had worn into the hospital. There was a ring. It didn't look like it was worth much. His old watch was in the bag, and so was his wallet. There was nothing in the wallet, no money, not a single piece of identification. I looked inside his coat and found a letter he had been carrying.

It was a letter from me. I had written it six months before. It was short, maybe a page, type-written. Down at the end, I had given him some grief about straightening out his life. I told him I would have to think twice about inviting him to my house again if he didn't promise he wouldn't show up drinking. I'd just signed my name. I didn't say "love" or anything. I had just signed my god-damned name like I was a real hardass.

I still wonder why he carried such a letter around with him for so long. Maybe he kept it as a re-minder to do better. I don't know. Maybe he kept it to remind himself his only son was turning on him. Whatever, I never forgave myself for that letter. I can't get it out of my head he died not knowing how much I loved him.

I'd held back most of the tears until I had reached the part about the letter. Then they came full force.

"Dammit!" I said to my friend. "I can't help cry-ing when I talk about that."

I lifted my head from my hands and noticed my friend was crying too.

"I still miss my daddy, too," he sobbed. "Just two weeks before he went in the hospital, I was sup-posed to take him fishing. I called him and told him

I had too much to do at the office. He loved to fish, and I put him off because I was too damn busy."

"You never stop loving your daddy," I said.

"No matter what," said my friend.

Together, we had reached the stage of "CRYIN'-ABOUT-YOUR-DADDY DRUNK," two grown men, bellies full of beer, sobbing about the memories of their late fathers.

Soon, we would be reaching "INVISIBLE," so we popped one more cold beer and toasted our precious memories. Before my friend's wife came and put us to bed—"Bull-sheyet," I said to his wife, "gimme them keys. I can drive"—my friend said to me, "Know what I would do if I were you, a writer? I'd write a book about my old man. I'd write about how much I loved him, about how much he meant to me."

I said nobody would want to read about me and my daddy.

"At least you'd feel better about it all," said my friend.

I've been CAYDD a number of times since then, and hardly an episode passed that I didn't think about that book, a book about Daddy, about his life and his hard times, about how much I loved him and how much he meant to me. About how I still miss him and about how I'm forty years old and I'm still crying for him.

I mentioned the idea of a book to a relative once, who said, "Forget the book. Put him behind you. It's over. That was another part of your life. Forget the book and forget him."

But I couldn't do that. I have his name. When I

look at pictures of him, I can see my resemblance to him. I can do his voice. I can *sound* like him, especially when I tell one of his stories, and I tell them often.

He was a hero. He was a drunk. He was a con artist. He made my cry. He made me laugh. I loved him with all my heart.

There is a title to this book out there on the cover somewhere. But don't go by that. From the start, I've called this *My Daddy Book.*

I just thought I'd feel a lot better if I wrote it.

CHAPTER
2

I NEVER HAVE SERIOUSLY LOOKED INTO MY FAMILY ON MY daddy's side. I go back only as far as his daddy, my paternal grandfather. Frankly, I've never been interested in that sort of thing. Besides, I recall the Rodney Dangerfield line, "I looked up my family tree and found out I was the sap."

I do know something of the origin of the family name, however. One day, I was thumbing through the paper and came to one of those "Know Your Name" features. "Grizzard," believe it or not, was in there.

"Grizzard," said the article, is from the French *gris,* which means "gray." "Grissard," which is how the French spell my name, translates as "codger" or "old, gray-headed man."

Needless to say, I was disappointed by all this. I didn't mind being of French origin, but "codger" and "old gray-headed man"? Somehow, I would have expected "Grizzard" to be French, or whatever, for "wild stallion" or something like that.

There are two ways to pronounce my last name. My family has always pronounced it "Griz-*zard*," the last syllable rhyming with "lard." Others with the same last name, however, pronounce it "Grizzerd," as in "lizard" or "blizzard." I find this pronunciation most unappealing. How anybody with a perfectly lovely French name could pronounce it as if it were some sort of chicken part is beyond me. If "Griz-*zard*" meant "wild stallion," I once decided, then "Griz-zerd" must certainly translate as "sissy, welfare recipient."

It is puzzling to me why most people, upon seeing my last name in print, inevitably will go for the "Griz-zerd" as in "lizard" or "blizzard" pronunciation. I've been paged at a lot of important places, such as bus stations and various drinkeries, and the call is always for Lewis "Griz-zerd." My first day in high school, the principal was calling out names for homeroom assignments. When he came to my name, he stuttered, he stumbled and then, sure as hell, he sent Lewis "Griz-zerd" to Miss Ruth Young's freshman homeroom. My friends all thought that was hilarious.

This has continued into my adulthood. People think it is funny, and quite original, to pronounce my last name, "Griz-zerd," or "gizzard." I consider these people doo-doo pots who do not love the Lord. (I must admit, however, that often, while looking over menus, I have been startled by the offering of "French-Fried Chicken Gizzards, $4.95," which is only one letter from being even more startling. Also, a reader once sent along a receipt she had received from a grocery store. The receipt stated she had paid $1.19 for "Turkey Grizzards." The reader found great amusement in this. I found none.)

Something else. Now that I have my own newspaper column and have appeared twice on "Nashville Now," people suggest that I have changed my name from "Griz-zerd" to "Griz-*zard*," as Tony "Dor-*sett*" changed his to "*Dor*-set." Or was it the other way around?

That is absolutely not true. My family always has pronounced our last name "Griz-*zard*," even those members of the family who were horse thieves and later became Presbyterians.

Something else I have had to listen to all my life is a joke that half the population of the free world has told me, the infamous "Mr. Rab-*bit*" joke, which I offer here only as an example of what I have had to endure:

Mr. Turtle, Mr. Buzzard, and Mr. Rabbit decided to build themselves a beautiful new home. They built an absolute mansion. As the finishing touches were being added, however, they noticed the grounds were a mess. Mr. Turtle and Mr. Buzzard suggested Mr. Rabbit go and fetch some fertilizer for the subsequent groundskeeping.

Mr. Rabbit left on the long journey to find the fertilizer. Six weeks later, he returned. He was greeted at the front door of the new mansion by a stuffy butler.

"With whom would you like to speak?" asked the butler.

"Mr. Turtle," said the rabbit.

"I'm sorry," replied the butler, "but Mr. Tur-*tell* is out by the well."

"Okay," said Mr. Rabbit, "then I'd like to speak to Mr. Buzzard."

"I'm sorry," said the butler, "but Mr. Buz-*zard* is out in the yard."

"Fine," said Mr. Rabbit. "Just tell 'em that Mr. Rab-*bit* is here with the shit."

The only amusing story I've heard involving the mispronunciation of my last name—or someone who mispronounces it—came from my friend Dr. Ferrol Sams, country doctor, marvelous storyteller, and author of two successful novels, *Run with the Horsemen* and *Whisper of the River*.

Dr. Sams informed me there was once a Dr. Griz-zerd (as in "lizard," etc.) in his hometown of Fayetteville, Georgia. Dr. Griz-zerd's wife had a poodle dog of which she was quite fond. One day Mrs. Griz-zerd attached a note to her fluffy white poodle that said, "I'm Dr. Griz-zerd's little dog, whose little dog are you?" and sent the poor dog out in town to make new friends.

Unfortunately for the dog, it proceeded to waltz into the local pool hall where several members of the town's sporting crowd gathered each day.

Some moments later, the dog returned to Mrs. Griz-zerd's waiting arms, obviously in terrible distress. Upon further inspection, Mrs. Griz-zerd, according to Dr. Sams, saw a new note attached to it, which asked the musical question, "I've got turpentine in my little ass, what have you got in yours?"

I know there are people with my last name in

Alabama, in Tennessee, and in Virginia, although I imagine I would only be quite distantly related to most of them.

Once I was driving through east Alabama and I came upon an old store that obviously had closed long ago. On the side of the building, above the words "Jefferson Island Salt" was painted "Grizzard's Store." I stopped at a nearby house and asked, "Are the people who ran Grizzard's Store still around?"

"Ain't nobody here by that name," I was told.

I, of course, realized my mistake.

"They must have pronounced it 'Griz-zerd,'" I said.

"Reckin they said it like it was spelt," was the rather tart response.

I drove away in a huff. No wonder the stupid store went out of business.

On another occasion, I was driving through Tullahoma, Tennessee. I was stopped at a red light and noticed I was at the intersection of "Grizzard Street." Immediately, I went in search of more information, stopping at a nearby service station.

"Ain't no 'Griz-*zards*' around here," said a man with grease on his nose. "But they's plenty of 'Griz-zerds.'" I naturally didn't bother to look any of them up.

It was my pleasure once to sit with the actor George Grizzard, whose forebears were from Virginia. He was in Atlanta doing a play. He, to my great relief, pronounces his last name as I do. We sat and sipped and talked ugly about the "Griz-zerds," most of whom likely live in trailer parks.

All I know about my family is my paternal grandfather, Augustus Adolphus Grizzard, was reared in Gwinnett County, Georgia, and that he married Eugenia McDonald, also of Gwinnett County, and they had twelve children. My father, Lewis McDonald Grizzard, was the youngest of those twelve.

Both my paternal grandfather and grandmother died before I was born, which I have always considered a shame. From talking to relatives and those who knew my grandparents, I know that my grandmother was a tiny and gentle woman who spoiled all her sons.

My grandfather, known as "A.A." or "Mr. Dolph," was musically inclined and led all the singing at the Zoar Methodist Church, some few miles outside Snellville, Georgia, then barely a speck in the road, now a bedroom community to Atlanta with a Kroger store that sells live lobsters.

The only photograph of my paternal grandparents is one from an Atlanta newspaper that appeared on the occasion of their fiftieth wedding anniversary.

My grandfather looked like a man inclined to music. He looked like a man who enjoyed laughter, an assumption that was confirmed by a man who introduced himself to me at a social gathering one evening by saying he, as a boy, had known my grandfather.

"Mr. Dolph was a fine man," he began. "And Lord, he could sing. He'd bring the rafters down at church on Sunday mornings."

My father got his penchant for loud church singing honestly, then.

"I'll tell you what I remember most about your
granddaddy, though," the man continued. "He
could bray like a mule. I never heard nothing like it
in my life. Mr. Dolph could do a mule better'n a
mule could do hisself.

"He'd go [I have no idea how to write how a
mule sounds, so be content with the fact if I could
write it, there would likely be a lot of *e*'s.], and I
mean you'd swear you were hearing the real thing."

A man, upon hearing that his grandfather left,
among his other legacies, the fact he could make
wonderful mule sounds, must consider further just
what that means, in relation to not only his grandfather, but to his father, his uncles, and even to
himself.

For instance, I wonder how my grandfather, Mr.
Dolph, learned to make mule sounds? I suppose it
was because he was a hard-working man who
plowed a million miles of Georgia red clay behind
his mule. Out there alone with the beast, he was
likely to form at least some line of communication,
one would think. Naturally, the mule wasn't going
to turn around to my grandfather and ask, "What's
for dinner tonight?" so it was left up to my grandfather to speak to the mule in mule talk.

This leads me to believe my grandfather must
have been a man of great patience and understanding to lower himself to a mule's level of communication. Of course, except for the church, there really
weren't many means of entertaining one's self in
Gwinnett County in those days, and perhaps my

grandfather could find no other recreation besides perfecting his mule impression.

As far as the rest of the family is concerned, I don't think any of us inherited this ability. God knows, I hope none of my aunts did. Making mule sounds certainly could set a girl back a ways.

My father could do dogs and cats. I recall he was a riot doing both species when I was a small child sitting in his lap, but I never heard him do a mule.

I can do a donkey. My college roommate taught me to do that. You whistle real loud and then holler "Haw!" to do a donkey. It's also got all those *e*'s.

I suppose, then, the mule thing ended with my grandfather, which is just as well. The mule has been replaced by the tractor, anyway, and people who specialize in agricultural sounds today do tractors and threshers and pickup trucks. This has absolutely nothing to do with the rest of this book, but I went to school with a kid who did the best pickup truck ever.

He could do trying to crank a pickup truck on a cold morning:

"Udennnnn, udennnnn, udennnnn."

He would then do all the sounds of a truck while its gears were being shifted? (low) Udennnnn, (second) udennnnnn, (high) *"udennnnnn!"*

The child, one of the Jones boys, whom we nicknamed "Uden-Uden," was so into truck sounds that somewhere in the middle of the fifth grade, he actually came to think he *was* a truck and ceased making any intelligible sounds other than uden-udens, which put somewhat of a burden on teachers who were trying to educate him.

"Who was the fourth president of the United States?" the teacher asked Uden-Uden one day.

Uden did trying to crank a pickup on a cold morning and the teacher sent him to see the principal. The principal, in turn, sent a letter home to Uden-Uden's parents indicating he had become somewhat of a difficult case, and if he did not cool it with the truck sounds, then he would suffer the consequences of a sound thrashing.

"You think you've got problems with him?" Uden-Uden's mother wrote back to the principal. "At home, he won't drink his milk unless it's poured into an empty can of Quaker State. And last week he claimed he couldn't do his chores because his manifold was busted."

Later, Uden-Uden realized he could not go through his life as a truck, and he straightened out. Last I heard of him he was working as a mechanic at a Shell station and had three sons named Chevy, Ford, and little Lug Nut, the baby.

But back to my father's family.

My grandmother, the former Eugenia McDonald, was, by all descriptions, especially fond of her baby, Lewis, whom she dressed in knickers until he was twelve and who never had a haircut until he was the same age because his mother didn't want to snip away his blond curls. Little Lewis didn't mind the knickers or the curls and he certainly didn't want his mama to be disappointed, but the daily beatings at school and the fact he was mistaken for a girl by one of his teachers and forced to dance with a boy while his class was learning the Virginia reel was quite hard on him. He finally pleaded with his mother to allow him to wear regular pants and have his hair cut.

I didn't know all my aunts and uncles. Some of them died before I was born, too. The fact my mother and father were divorced when I was six and I lived with my mother afterward cut down the time I spent around my aunts and uncles on my father's side, but I knew them to be a lively bunch with the one trait that seemed to have run through the Grizzard strain, a marvelous sense of humor and a certain zest for life.

Aunt Essie was the oldest. She died when I was quite young. She was up in her seventies. She married a man named Pleasant David Rawlins, who was a railroad man. They lived near the tracks in Clarkson, Georgia, just outside Atlanta, and when I went to see them, Uncle Pleas would tell me train stories while Aunt Essie was busy in the kitchen making her specialty, roast pork with fresh vegetables out of Uncle Pleas's garden.

When I spent the night with Aunt Essie and Uncle Pleas, I was comforted by the sounds of trains passing in the night. I also remember that Uncle Pleas passed a great deal of gas throughout the night, and I spent many an evening marveling at his range before I drifted off to sleep.

My Aunt Jessie was a sweet lady. Her husband died young and she took to running the Atlanta Women's Club on Peachtree Street. When my father fell on hard times after Korea and after his army career folded, Aunt Jessie would lend him money and fuss about his drinking.

"You know that stuff will kill you, Lewis," she said to him.

"Not in front of *him*," my father said to his sister, gesturing toward me. I was eight or nine.

"He's the reason you need to stop drinking," scolded my Aunt Jessie. "He's what you've got to live for."

If my Aunt Jessie had been around my father all the time, she might have pulled him away from the bottle. At least, that's what I like to think.

My Aunt Mary was a nurse. She died of cancer. What I remember most about her was that she had a great deal of patience and taught me how to play Canasta.

My Uncle Walt and my Uncle John Wesley were in the used-car business. They ran Grizzard Motors in Atlanta and Uncle Walt told me once about selling a bunch of cars one afternoon and then taking the profits to buy a room at the Henry Grady Hotel downtown.

"We had a fine time, yes we did," said my Uncle John Wesley in his deep, distinctive voice.

"We ordered up a couple of thick steaks and bought us some good whiskey and had a man from Muse's bring over a rack of suits so we could pick out what we wanted without having to leave the hotel room. Come Monday morning, we didn't have a dime left—not a dime—but we had a full belly and suits finer than any preacher ever wore."

One of our distant cousins did a spot on the infamous "$64,000 Question" television quiz show and made a bundle answering questions on the Civil War. We are not certain if she received any coaching before her appearance, as others did, but one thing she did with her money was leave her home in Virginia and come to visit her relatives in Georgia. Nobody was certain quite how it happened, but when she left to return home, she and her husband went back in separate cars they had purchased from Walt and John Wesley, who were back at the Henry Grady eating steaks and picking out suits again.

I'm not saying Walt and John Wesley were anything but as up front and honest as used car dealers can afford to be, but as my father once said, "I love Walt and I love John Wesley. They are my brothers. But I'd never buy a car from either one of them."

My Uncle Frank was perhaps the most classic of all the Grizzard brothers. He was a stout man, who wore spats and straw bowlers and who became one of the city's most celebrated criminal attorneys.

They still tell the story at certain law school commencements about when Uncle Frank was practicing law back during the Depression.

Uncle Frank had this office in downtown Atlanta, but he had few clients, the times being as hard as they were. Mostly, Uncle Frank would report to work with a bottle of Four Roses and spend the day with that.

One afternoon, however, a young man walked in and announced, "I am looking for the famous criminal attorney, Frank B. Grizzard."

Uncle Frank peered over his glasses and said, "My good man, you have the honor of addressing the famous criminal attorney Frank B. Grizzard. Now, what can I do for you?"

"Are you as good an attorney as people say?"

"Son," answered Uncle Frank, "south of Richmond, Virginia, I have no peer."

"Well," said the man, "I am expecting to be charged with murder in the not-too-distant future, and I want to know what it costs to retain an attorney of your class and reputation."

"To have me beside you in a court of law, my boy, it would cost you ten thousand dollars and not one penny less."

The man hung his head and began to leave Uncle Frank's office. "I am afraid," he said, "I could not begin to pay such a fee. I do not have that kind of money."

As the man began to walk away, Uncle Frank said, "Now, just a minute. How much do you have?"

"I have three hundred dollars in the bank," he answered.

"My good man," said Uncle Frank, "you have just retained the services of criminal attorney, nonpareil, Frank B. Grizzard. And from this day forward, never let it be said that I am a man to quibble over a few dollars."

My father took me to see Uncle Frank try a case one afternoon. He died soon afterward, and I will forever be thankful for the opportunity to have seen him work.

He was defending a man charged with making moonshine.

"The defense will stipulate that my client made a little illegal whiskey," Uncle Frank began his summation to the jury, "but just enough to keep body and soul together."

As Uncle Frank spoke, a woman sitting in the row behind the defense table began to cry, wailing louder and louder as Uncle Frank pleaded with the jury harder and harder.

Sure enough, the jury found Uncle Frank's client innocent. As we left the courtroom my father said to Uncle Frank, "That man's wife was pitiful."

Uncle Frank said, "Wife? What wife?"

"The one who did all the crying," my father said.

"That wasn't his wife," said Uncle Frank. "That was just some ol' gal I paid fifty dollars to come heah and squall."

Although she was not blood kin, some mention also should be made about Uncle Frank's wife, Aunt Emily. When Uncle Frank met her, she was a teller of fortunes and was believed to have certain magical powers. Or, at least that is what she convinced her wealthy clients of. It was once rumored in the family that Aunt Emily—Uncle Frank called her "Jilly-Willy"—had over a million dollars hidden somewhere on Uncle Frank's property, a place south of Atlanta known as Grizzard Ranch, on the basis that Uncle Frank bought his adopted daughter a horse that Aunt Jilly-Willy would never let the daughter ride because the horse was pregnant. The fact the horse was pregnant several years without ever producing a foal never deterred Aunt Jilly-Willy from disallowing her daughter or any visiting cousins to ride the horse.

Aunt Jilly-Willy talked very fast. And she talked all the time. When Uncle Frank would get enough, he would say, "In the name of God, woman, won't you please just hush?" Aunt Jilly-Willy would ig-

nore his pleas and continue to ramble on with gusts
up to fifty miles per hour.

I was visiting once and Uncle Frank was playing
cards with several of his friends. Aunt Jilly-Willy
walked into the room with a Chihuahua puppy.

"In the name of God, woman," he said, "where
did you get that little dog?"

"At the pet store, Frank, at the pet store."

"How much did the little fella cost?" Uncle Frank
went on.

"Five hundred dollars, Frank, five hundred dollars." (When Aunt Jilly-Willy couldn't think of
anything else to say, she would repeat what she had
just said, sometimes five or six times.)

Uncle Frank was aghast. "You mean to say you
spent five hundred dollars on a little dog no bigger'n a minute?" he asked.

"Frank, Frank, Frank," Aunt Jilly-Willy began, "I
got the dog because our daughter has asthma and
everybody knows Chihuahua dogs cure asthma,
Frank."

Uncle Frank put his cards down and peered over
his glasses at the others around the table and spoke
in an aside, as if his wife weren't there.

"Every year," he began, "this country spends
millions of dollars to educate the heathen all over
this world. And to think," he added, nodding toward Aunt Jilly-Willy, "we have such vast igno-
rance in our own midst."

After Uncle Frank died, Aunt Jilly-Willy wanted
to move away from Grizzard Ranch, so she sold the
place to another nephew, who decided to renovate
it. While the workers were there one day, Aunt

Jilly-Willy returned to get a few things she had left behind, and she casually mentioned to the workers she had buried several thousand dollars' worth of gold on the property and had forgotten where it was.

When the new owner dropped by later, he found each worker with a pair of post hole diggers, looking for gold in his backyard.

"There wasn't a sprig of grass left that hadn't been uprooted," is how he remembers the incident.

Nobody every found the gold, incidentally, and nobody knows whatever happened to Aunt Jilly-Willy, either. I lived in constant fear she would come to see me in my workplace and embarrass me beyond belief, but she never did. The last we heard of her, she was living with a dentist, driving a pink Cadillac convertible, and carrying a portable radio at her ear wherever she went. She had to be at least eighty when all that took place, and perhaps the one thing she did for her country is plant the seed from whence the ghetto blaster idea sprouted.

My Aunt Rufy is the only member of the Grizzard family still living. She and Uncle Harry still live in the same house where I visited them as a child. They had two daughters and a son. The son was killed in an automobile accident. One daughter, Mickey, had red hair and would take me along on her movie dates, much to the chagrin, I am certain, of her male companions. The other daughter, Mary Jean, was, and still is, quite beautiful. I think one of the reasons I have had difficulty in staying married (I have divorced three wives and am currently auditioning for a fourth) is because I never could find anybody just like my cousin Mary Jean. She, incidentally, is the one who told me to forget the idea about writing a book about Daddy. She was the victim of one of my crying-about-your-daddy drunk spells one night over long-distance telephone. I later apologized for the incident, and she understood. When she reads this, I hope she will also understand why I ignored her advice.

The first forty years of being a Grizzard has been worth it, I think. I've had trouble with a world full of comedians thinking it was hilarious to mispronounce my name, but I have learned to deal with that. Grizzard is not the kind of name that is easily forgotten, either, and because the professor sat us in alphabetical order in a journalism course I had in college, I was able to sit next to the prettiest girl enrolled at the University of Georgia at the time because her name also began with a G. I never spoke to the girl the entire quarter because I was afraid to (I have some of my mother's people's blood in me, too, and her family was quite conservative). But when I was in the hospital following heart surgery, I received a letter from that very same girl and she said she remembered me quite well and reads the things I write. I could have kicked myself for not making some kind of move on her twenty years ago, but at least I now have her letter acknowledging she actually knew I existed back then when I was sure she considered me—a skinny kid with thick glasses wearing high-water pants and white socks—a non-person.

Because I write books and newspaper articles that

are attempts at being humorous, people often ask me where I got the ability to be funny.

That's easy. I got it from my daddy's side of the family. I got it from Daddy. Even at a very young age, I could tell the difference between my father's family and my mother's.

I love my aunts and my uncles and my cousins on my mother's side. My maternal grandparents raised me and I loved them with all my heart.

But they were quiet and spent a lot of time sitting under trees discussing the weather and who died recently. They were hard-working people, deeply religious, who warned me of the hellfire of my streak of laziness that kept me from any interest in things I didn't enjoy doing, such as working in the fields where one tended to get very hot and dirty.

My mother's side of the family hated alcohol with a fierce passion. The Grizzards would take a drink and they would sing and they would dance and they would tell funny stories.

My daddy, even when his times were hardest, was never without a joke to tell some stranger he'd met thirty seconds earlier. I admit I am still stealing his material, still using characters that he forged first.

There was Lucille Wellmaker, a stout girl with whom my father went to school. She wore "bermuda-alls," overalls cut off at the knee, and carried a wagon spoke to dances. If anybody refused to dance with her, in my daddy's words, she would "turn the whole place out with that wagon spoke."

There was Hester Camp, who was uglier than an

empty glass of buttermilk, and there was Ollie Groves, who used to ride a pig to school.

And there were his jokes. God, I still remember them and when I tell them again, often I fall into my father's voice. I do a magnificent impression of my father's voice:

There was this ol' boy who up and died, and he had loved to eat cheese all his life. His wife decided she'd put a big piece of limburger cheese in the casket with him.

These two friends of his were looking down at the ol' boy in the casket and they didn't know about the cheese. One of 'em up and said, "Lord, Lord, he looks like he could just up and talk."

The other, gettin' a whiff of that two-day-old cheese, said, "If he did what I think he just did, he'd better say, 'Excuse me.'"

Then there were the two preachers:

There was this small town with a Baptist and a Methodist church. Both congregations had young preachers and they both rode bicycles to the services every Sunday morning, and every Sunday morning they would meet and exchange notes.

One morning, the Baptist preacher walked up on foot. The Methodist preacher said, "Brother, where is your bicycle?"

The Baptist preacher said, "Brother, I believe somebody in my congregation has stolen my bicycle."

The Methodist minister was appalled. He said, "I'll tell you how to get your bicycle back. You preach on the Ten Commandments this morning and when you get to 'Thou Shalt Not Steal' you bear down on it. You make 'em feel that fire, smell that brimstone! Whoever stole your bicycle will start feeling bad and bring it back to you.''

The Baptist preacher said he'd try it. The next Sunday morning, sure enough, he was on his bicycle again.

''Hallelujah!'' shouted the Methodist minister. ''I see you preached on the Ten Commandments and got your bicycle back. I'll bet you had the thief really squirming when you bore down on 'Thou Shalt Not Steal.'

''Well, that's not exactly what happened,'' said the Baptist minister.

''What do you mean?'' asked the Methodist preacher.

''Well, I did preach on the Ten Commandments,'' his colleague said, ''but when I got to 'Thou Shalt Not Commit Adultery,' I remembered where I left my bicycle.''

He was a great people-watcher, my daddy. He saw funny where no one else would. He laughed at skinny, "wormy" men he'd see on the streets. Because the Grizzards were a rather large-in-the-waist group, whenever he'd see a fat woman, he would say, "I believe there's one of the Grizzard girls." He never met a waitress he didn't call "Pearl."

Whenever he walked into a place to make a purchase and was not immediately waited on, he would offer up, in a loud, high-pitched voice, "I'm leav-*ing.*" He once walked into a restaurant with a large appetite and noticed it said, "All the fried chicken you can eat, $3.95."

He called the waitress over.

"Pearl," he said, "is the management of this establishment prepared to back up this claim of all the fried chicken I can eat for $3.95?"

She said that it was.

"Then, dear woman," he said, "please alert the management that they are about to be in serious financial trouble."

The man could eat. God, how he could eat, especially after he returned from Korea, after nearly starving to death when his outfit practically was wiped out at Unsan. He'd been kept alive on rice for two weeks by a Chinese soldier who apparently wanted to desert. Years ago, I was much heavier myself, and my fat face looked even more like his than it does today.

He loved fried chicken. He also loved country ham and homemade biscuits and he used to buy those sausages he called "red-hots," which he would fry for a late snack. He ate what he called a "Snellville milkshake," cornbread soaking in a glass of buttermilk. One thing that was not passed down from my father to me was his affinity for buttermilk.

But I do have his voice. I also got his love for a funny story. And his love for great characters, great one-liners. I got his love of being the center of attention and with that the ability and material to have them rolling in the aisles.

I got his love for his country.

I am forty years old. I have been married and divorced three times and I don't have any children. The problem is that there was only one other male offspring from my father's family, and he is older than me, and he has only daughters, so if I do not come through with a son, then there is the distinct possibility the Grizzard name—or at least my father's family's use of it for quite a while—will end.

That is an awesome responsibility as I see it, and you know how those of us from the South can be about our family names.

I suppose I would like to have a son, or my ego would. I have fantasized about it over the years. I probably would name him Lewis McDonald Grizzard, III. Maybe he would be known as "Little Lewis" and I would be "Big Lewis." We would go to ball games together and I would tell him stories like my father told me. And when he asked me about his grandfather, I would sit back and sigh and become wistful and say, "He was a great American, son. You would have loved him, and he would have loved you."

Maybe he would grow up enjoying laughter and could pass it on to others. Maybe he would honor me, by using my material, as I have used my father's. Whatever talent I have, Daddy was the foundation of it.

Something like that would be nice to pass down a second time.

CHAPTER
3

BASKETBALL HAS BEEN AN IMPORTANT PART OF MY LIFE. I
played it on the playground level, the junior high
level, the high school level, and I played recreation
league basketball during my college days.

I wanted to play college basketball because I
wanted to impress my father. He had taken me to
my first college game when I was eight. We watched
Georgia Tech play Kentucky.

"Work hard enough on your game," he told me,
"and maybe one day you could be as good as the
boys on the Tech and Kentucky teams."

I took him at his word and I quickly took on
basketball as my life's work. We did not have a
gymnasium at the school in Moreland where I attended the second through the eighth grades. We
had two outdoor baskets that had been erected on
the sloping playground.

The basket on the higher end of the playground

was easily the better of the two goals. The one on the lower end was a foot or so shorter than the other end, and because rainwater tends to flow downhill, the lower court had gullies, making it quite difficult to get a true dribble.

The rule on the playground at school was simple: the older boys, the better players, of course, used the upper court and the younger boys played on the lower. Usually, one could expect to move to the upper goal upon reaching the seventh grade. May I say it remains one of the great accomplishments of my life that I was allowed on upper court games in the fifth grade because of my gifted shooting eye.

The following summer I attended Camp Thunder, the district Boy Scout camp. There was a gymnasium at Camp Thunder and while others were out studying nature and tying knots, I was in basketball heaven.

Soon, my reputation as a player spread through the camp. I took on all comers in One-on-One, Horse, and Twenty-one, a game involving the art of shooting free throws, at which I had no peer.

One day, some of the campers from a rival cabin came to the gymnasium and said they had somebody who could destroy me. His name was Harkness—I will never forget that name—and he played on the B team at his local high school. Harkness was thirteen, several inches taller and much stronger than I.

We began with a friendly game of Horse. Harkness said I could go first. A crowd had gathered to watch this epic struggle.

I began with a couple of left-handed layups to see what he had. Harkness made them both.

Then, I went to ten feet and made a couple of jumpers. Harkness made those, too. So he could play a lick. I went to my *A* material.

I hit one from the corner. Harkness's shot rimmed out. *H*.

I nailed one from the top of the circle. Harkness hit the front of the rim. *HO*.

I came back with another left-handed layup. I could sense he was becoming frustrated by the fact I had made six straight shots.

Harkness missed his shot. *HOR*.

I banked in a John Havlicek, a fourteen-footer from the left side of the basket. Harkness missed. *HORS*.

I went to the free-throw line after that. A lot of people make mistakes when they play Horse, by not going to the shot they know they will never miss. It puts tremendous pressure on the opponent when he sees you own a certain shot.

It was after my sixth free throw that Harkness finally missed and was out of the game.

"Why don't you whip his ass?" said one of Harkness's fellow campers. I had hoped he wouldn't think of such a thing, but it was the custom of the day that if you got beat at anything, you immediately started a fight.

Harkness let me have one on the left side of my head, then threw the basketball down to the other end of the court and disappeared into the woods.

I took my basketball seriously—and I took an occasional physical beating—because one day I wanted to play the game in front of my father. He had been a basketball player, too. As a matter of fact, in researching his youth, most people mention first that my father could play the game.

"Had the best two-handed set shot in the county," somebody said.

"Lord, Lewis could flat play basketball," said somebody else.

I even discovered that he played high school ball well into his twenties.

"See, what he'd do," said an old classmate, "is graduate from one school and then enroll in another the next year as a senior. There wasn't much checking around about eligibility in those days, and he just kept on playing. I think they finally got on to him up in Rabun County, though, because he looked so much older than his coach."

He became a teacher before the war, my daddy, and did some coaching. He even enjoyed coaching girls' basketball. I hated girls' basketball. Girls can't jump.

"We were playing this game one night and the gym was packed," he told me. "I had this big ol' girl from out in the country on my team. Lord, she was mean. She hit a referee square on the mouth one night when he called a foul on her. Put 'im out cold is what I mean.

"Anyway, we're playing a game and Big Bertha— that's what I called her—was dribbling down the court. It was one of those moments when everybody in the gym was sort of quiet. She dribbled the ball off her foot and it went out of bounds.

"I can still hear her today. She put her hands on

her hips and said, 'Sheyet fahr!' I laughed 'til I thought I would die."

My father coached basketball in the military as well. Before the whiskey got him and the army gave him his walking papers, he was athletic officer at Fort Benning, soon after he returned from Korea.

One of the bright memories of the few years I lived with both my parents was sitting on the bench with Daddy while he coached basketball. One of the dark memories of that time is that is how I came to have the despicable nickname "Skippy."

The players referred to my father as "Skipper." When I came along, they referred to me as Skippy. I grew to hate the name. I had fights in school over it. I pleaded with my mother and other members of my family not to call me by that name. I was Lewis, I said. Skippy is something you name a dog or a pet duck.

By the time I was twelve, most of my family had ceased on the Skippy thing. Everybody but my maternal grandmother.

"You will always be Skippy to me," she said. And I was. She was still calling me that when she died. I was well into my thirties at the time. I was thinking at her funeral that Skippy had died with my grandmother. I said to myself that Skippy probably wasn't that bad a nickname after all.

I made the junior high team when I was in the seventh grade at Moreland School. We did quite well against other teams in the county, considering the fact we had to play all our games away and couldn't practice when it was raining or when it was so cold the nets on the playground courts froze.

We even came in second in the county tournament and won a trophy. In the semifinals, we played Arnco-Sargent School, from a mill town, and our coach, who was just out of college, decided to freeze the ball after we achieved a 2–0 lead and got the ball back. He noticed all our opponents ran a zone defense and his idea was to freeze the ball until Arnco-Sargent had to abandon the zone and play us man-for-man.

We froze the ball until two minutes to go in the game when we still had the 2–0 lead. Arnco-Sargent came out of their zone and we won something like 6–3. In the finals we played East Coweta and we were freezing the ball again until I threw it away. We lost and our coach broke his hand slamming it against the bench when I threw the ball away. Later he became a Baptist minister and, presumably, forgave me.

In the ninth grade, students from Moreland and other parts of Coweta County were bused into the county seat of Newnan and Newnan High School. Rarely did someone from one of the county schools make it in athletics at Newnan.

Newnan kids, the city kids, had been playing organized sports for years while I was trying to learn to dribble through gullies and ravines.

There was another problem as well. Newnan was seven miles from Moreland. I wasn't old enough to drive at fourteen and, even if I had been, I wouldn't have had a car.

Basketball practice ended after the bus for More-land had been gone for a couple of hours.

"You mean you have to practice every day?" my mother asked.

Mothers are great but most of them know little or nothing about basketball.

"There is no way I can come get you every day," my mother, who taught fifth grade at the Moreland School, said.

"As soon as I get home, I have to get supper for you and H.B. [my stepfather]."

I was sobbing.

"I want to be a basketball player like Daddy," I said, between the tears.

"It means a lot to you, doesn't it, son?" my mother asked.

I sobbed out a "Yes, ma'am."

"Well, we'll do something," she said, and I hugged her. I think she cried some, too. Mothers may not know a lot about basketball, but they do know a lot about little boys' dreams.

I made the B-team at Newnan High. I got myself a hand-me-down uniform from the varsity and I took it home and spread it out on my bed. There was a white, pull-over warm-up jacket with NEWNAN in block letters across it. There was a blue jersey and blue shorts, both of which were trimmed in gold. And there were blue and gold basketball stockings and everybody got his own personal jock-strap and a pair of black and white, low-cut basket-ball shoes, just like the Celtics wore. I stared at my uniform for hours when I got it home. Then I tried it on. Then I took it off. Then I tried it on again. I nearly wore out the mirror in my bedroom looking at myself.

I wanted to tell Daddy I had made the Newnan B-team basketball squad, but I didn't know where he was. He could do that. He would be some place with a "mahvelous" new job—he used "mahvelous" years before it became fashionable—and then I'd call and he would be gone and the person I talked to usually would mention Daddy owed him some money.

Once he was working as a cook in a hotel in Jackson, Georgia, thirty-five miles from Moreland. A former army officer with a brilliant war record, a cook in a hotel. One day I called him there.

"Your daddy's not at the hotel anymore," a lady told me.

"Do you know where he is?" I asked.

"Anybody know what happened to Lewis?" the woman asked somebody standing near her.

Before she could put her hand over the phone, a man's voice said, "I think they got him in jail down in Macon for passing bad checks."

The woman came back on the line and said, "I'm sorry, son, but I don't know where he went after he left here."

I thanked her and went to bed and cried. My daddy in jail.

Two weeks later, I got a call from him. He was somewhere in South Carolina with a "mahvelous" new job.

"Daddy," I said, "those people at the hotel where you worked before said you were in jail in Macon."

He laughed. "In the name of God, I wonder what made them say a thing like that?"

My first B-team game was at Headland High in suburban Atlanta. I hadn't heard from Daddy in a couple of months.

I didn't make the starting team for the first game, but we got way ahead, or way behind, I forget which, and the coach sent me along with the other reserves, into the game.

I was never much of a defensive player. Pure shooters like myself rarely are. I had sort of let the other four teammates go all the way down the court for defensive purposes, and when one of them grabbed a rebound, I was wide open.

The throw came to me, and I drove in for an easy layup, the first two points of my high school career. As I scored, I heard a voice from the stands that sounded familiar. I looked into the stands. I was astonished. It was Daddy. He had on a red baseball cap, with a whistle around his neck.

After the game was over, I hugged him and said, "Daddy, how did you know I was playing here?"

He said, "I am an instructor here."

"What do you instruct?"

"Physical education, Georgia history, and mechanical drawing."

"You don't know anything about mechanical drawing!"

"No, son," said Daddy, "but neither do my students."

I never made it to college ball for a couple of reasons. No college wants to sign a skinny kid who weighs 135 pounds and doesn't play defense. That, and when I did get my chance to impress a collegiate scout, I blew it.

We were playing my senior year and Whack Hyder, the basketball coach at Georgia Tech, had come to see a big center on the opposing team. Somebody casually mentioned Coach Hyder was in the stands as I dressed for the game.

This was it! My chance at college basketball! I broke out in a rash due to the excitement. I also forgot to put on my jock in a rush to get dressed.

I filled the air with jump shots that night. Unfortunately, very few of them went in the basket. As a matter of fact, I was something like 1-for-15 from the floor. The big center got 30 and we got drilled and Coach Hyder never said a word to me. For years I have blamed my poor shooting night on the fact I forgot to wear my athletic supporter. Once I discovered it was missing, I was so concerned with keeping my privates from showing, my shooting concentration was in serious trouble.

Daddy saw me play only once more after my first game at Headland. I was a junior. We were in the regional tournament against the top-ranked team in the state in our classification, a team that had already thrashed us soundly twice during the regular season.

That was twenty-four years ago. Nearly a quarter of a century later I remember every play, and, of course, every shot I made.

That was the night I had dreamed of. Big crowd. Big game. Daddy showed up as we were running up. He said he was just passing through and read in the papers that we were playing that night.

"Where have you been?" I asked him.

"I have this mahvelous job in [you name it]," he said.

I filled up the hoop. I had 20 points, mostly on fifteen- to twenty-footers over the opposition's zone, when the game ended in regulation time.

We went into overtime. The crowd was screaming. We got a basket. They got one. Score still tied. Then, they missed, and we hit a free throw. They scored to go one ahead again. Our coach called time. There were fifteen seconds to play.

Here was our plan: A teammate would toss the ball to me and I would dribble to the corner and get a pick from one of our forwards. I would take the last shot at a victory.

The buzzer sounded, calling time back in. I broke the wrong way for the toss-in and an opponent intercepted the ball. He was driving down the court for an uncontested layup that would put us three down and out of the game.

For some strange reason—having never had a thought concerning defense in my entire career—I went in pursuit of the opposing player. He went up for the layup and *missed.* Incredible, but he missed.

His momentum took him on under the basket and there I stood waiting for the rebound. As soon as I had the ball in my hands, I looked at the clock. Six seconds to play. All four of my teammates had their arms raised for a pass. I wasn't about to pass the ball.

I dribbled up the right side of the court, past two defenders and three of my teammates and just before the buzzer sounded, I threw up a six-foot bank shot that was mostly a prayer.

The ball went in the basket. My team had defeated the top-ranked team by one. My picture was in the Atlanta papers the next day. "Lithe Lewis Grizzard," said the caption. I still have that picture.

Suddenly there were people all over the court. They were screaming and cheering and throwing things. A fight or two broke out, I seem to recall. (Remember the old sports' maxim: When you lose, start a fight.)

My daddy found me in the mob.

"Mahvelous shot!" he bellowed, and he put his arms around me and squeezed me, and then he came along with the other parents who treated the team to a steak dinner.

I introduced him to everybody. After the dinner, one of my teammates' mother said to me, "My, but your father is such a debonair individual."

"He's smart, too," I replied. "One time he taught mechanical drawing."

Some of the old people over in Gwinnett County still talk about Daddy's ability as a musician and storyteller.

"When folks was sick back when yo' daddy was growin' up, when the doctor couldn't do no more for 'em, they'd call Lewis and he'd go over and play and sing and tell 'em a story or two. He saved 'bout as many as the doctors did."

He played the piano and he could make it talk. Make it *talk*. And he had that voice, that magnifi-

cent baritone that swept through church like a wind
gone wild.

"Ol' lady Mildred Dunn was sick most of her
life," went another story. "They done sent her all
the way to Atlanta to the hospital and nobody
would find out what her trouble was.

"She was a mean ol' woman, tell you the truth.
Never had married and that was most of her trouble, everybody thought. I bet that woman hadn't
smiled in thirty years when yo' daddy went to see
her one afternoon after church.

"Them that was there said he commenced to
singin' and playin' and Ol' lady Dunn got to toe
tappin' and beggin' him to play and sing more.

"He did and he started carryin' on a lot of his
foolishness with her and she started laughin' and
couldn't quit. Ol' lady Dunn lived another twenty
years and was spry as she could be after yo' daddy
paid her that visit."

My daddy sang mostly gospel music and he
played gospel piano. I don't think he really knew
how to read music or anything like that, but he
could fit his playing to almost any song.

He could make you cry with "The Old Rugged
Cross." He could bring you to your feet with "Revive Us Again."

He had this thing—a con, I suppose—he would
do in his later life when he traveled about, moving
from town to town, from job to job. He'd take a
teaching job at some small high school in late August and the first thing he would do afterward
would be to attend morning services at the local

Methodist church. I come from a long line of Meth-
odists.

He would take himself a seat down front—his
graying hair neatly cropped, wearing a starched
white shirt with, most times, a bow tie—and when
the singing would begin, he would, in the words he
used to describe Lucille Wellmaker and her habit of
starting a riot with a wagon spoke— "turn the place
out."

I saw him do it on a number of occasions:

"Now, brothers and sisters, let us turn our
hymnals (the Cokesbury, with the brown jacket) to
Number Ninety-five, 'I'm Dwelling in Beulah
Land,' and sing the first and last stanzas."

Daddy would boom it out:

> *O yes, I'm feasting on the manna*
> *From a boun-ti-ful supply,*
> *For I am dwelling*
> *In Beulah land.*

The murmurs would begin as soon as the singing
stopped.

"Who is that handsome man with that beautiful
voice?" one of the sisters would ask another.

After the service the members would flock to him
and he would be invited for Sunday dinner and
next week he would be asked to do a solo and after
that, the town belonged to him.

He never took anybody for a lot of money. He'd
get maybe a twenty from the preacher so he alleg-
edly could buy me new shoes before the school
term began. He might hit up the choir director for

ten and take a few bucks from the adoring widow lady. He would make his big score from the school principal anyway.

A week or so before teachers were supposed to report, he would visit the principal and mention he needed an advance on his first month's salary in order to find a place to live and purchase a few articles one must have to take up residence in a new place.

He was never denied. A couple of days before school was to begin, he would catch a bus out of town and never be heard from again. At least they had a few good Sundays of singing for their money and trouble.

I learned later that Daddy had discovered gospel singing could lead to great rewards at a young age. My Uncle Harry, Rufy's husband, told me the story:

"When ol' Lewis was just a boy—maybe about sixteen or seventeen—he and this friend of his decided they would hitchhike up to Chattanooga to see a couple of girls up there.

"Well, they got a ride as far as Calhoun when they got put out on the side of the road along about dark. They didn't have any money, and they were getting pretty tired and hungry.

"They thumbed for about an hour with no success. Then, they noticed this little church and saw a lot of people going inside. They decided there must be some kind of revival going on, and they went over to the church to see what it was all about.

"Well, the preacher welcomed everybody and

then said the piano player had become ill and couldn't be there for the first night of the revival.

"Ol' Lewis was sittin' in the back, and he got up —you know he never met a stranger—and said, 'I can play.' His friend stood up, too, and said, 'I can sing.'

"Well, the two of 'em went down to the front of the church and started playin' and singin' and the church just come apart. They had never heard such music before.

"After the services were over, several members of the congregation asked them if they could stay and bring the music all week. They said sure they could. So this family took 'em home and gave 'em some dinner and a bed. After the next night, another family took 'em home for the same things, and so on.

"After the week was out, Ol' Lewis and his friend went on to Chattanooga, bellies full of chickens and their pockets full of money."

Daddy never lost his love for gospel music. We are talking about Southern gospel quartet music that rocked and rolled in white frame churches and high school auditoriums long before Elvis.

When I spent time with him, we would usually make a ball game and a movie or two and at least one gospel singing. His favorite group was the "Lefevers," or as he described them, "The Mahvelous Lefevers."

They were a singing family and there was Urias and Alfus and Pierce and Mama Eva Mae, who played the piano. They were on an Atlanta television station for years on Sunday afternoons. I remembered who sponsored them. Martha White Self-Risin' Flour.

I talked to Eva Mae several years ago when her husband died. I told her how much my daddy had enjoyed their singing and playing. She sent me an autographed color photo, suitable for framing, of the Mah-velous Lefevers. It is a treasure.

Years after Daddy died, I went to Nashville on business and a friend took me over to the City Auditorium to the annual National Gospel Convention. There must have been a thousand Silver Eagle buses in the parking lot.

In the lobby of the auditorium were the booths of the various groups. Records. Tapes. T-shirts. Photographs. Inside, they were raising the roof with some good ol' "Wella, wella" music:

> *Wella, wella,*
> *ev'rybody's gonna have religion in glory,*
> *ev'rybody's gonna be singing that story,*
> *ev'rybody's gonna have a wonderful time up there,*
> *Oh, glory hallelujah . . .*

"Danged if that bass can't get down there and do it," I said to my friend.

"He can sing so low you can smell the shit on his breath."

I bought a tape when I left, the Mighty Kingsmen Quartet from Asheville. I listen to it when I am alone because there are very few people with whom I associate who are gospel music fans.

When I listen to "The Old Ship of Zion," I hear my daddy's voice in there somewhere, and I can see him, with his head rolled back, singing past all the others. There is a comfort in that.

My daddy was born on August 5, 1914. I know he graduated from Snellville High School and several other high schools, most likely, what with his continuing high school basketball career.

I know he spent a year or so as a student at the University of Georgia. He never graduated, but he did spend some time there. Later, he tried going into business for himself. He set up a hot dog stand (a "wienie joint," he called it) on the side of the road in Snellville.

That didn't last very long. What happened was one of his favorite stories.

"I was working and suddenly these two old girls came over the hill in a thirty-six Essex coupe. They lost control about the time they got to my little place of business and ran all up into my wienie joint."

"Anything left of it, Daddy?" I would ask, having heard the answer many times, but still enjoying it.

"Not an onion, son," he would say. "Not an onion."

He taught some school. I'm not sure what it took to get a teaching certificate in Georgia in the 1930s, but somehow Daddy talked himself into one.

He worked at Juhan's Fruit Store in Snellville, and he sold shirts in Atlanta, and while he was doing all this, he met a woman named Christine Word, my mother, from Carroll County.

The way Daddy always told it is that he first had met my Aunt Una in Atlanta and had asked her for a date. But when he arrived to pick her up, she wasn't home. Mother, Una's older sister, was sharing the apartment and she delivered the disappointing news to Daddy.

Undaunted, he asked, "What are *you* doing this evening?"

She had no plans, so off they went on their first date.

"He was the handsomest thing I'd ever seen," my mother would say years later. "He had all that black, curly hair and he could talk the ears off a donkey." (Which beats trying to impress her with an impression of one.)

Mother was a looker herself. I've seen pictures of her when she was in full-flowering youth. She was tall, and she had long, black hair. If it had been me instead of my daddy, I would have fallen for her mostly because of her eyes, a deep green set against that black hair. She had thin lips, but great shoulders. I don't know if anybody else but me notices shoulders on a woman, but I do. Bacall had great shoulders. I go for tall, boney women.

They got married, Mother and Daddy, in 1941. Then the Japanese bombed Pearl Harbor. The hell that would be the rest of Daddy's life had begun.

CHAPTER
4

A FEW YEARS AFTER DADDY DIED—I WAS WORKING FOR THE
Atlanta Journal sports department at the time—I was
home one day, sick with the flu. My telephone
rang. I got out of bed and answered it.

There was a man on the other end. He introduced
himself and said he was from someplace in Mary-
land and he was driving down to see his son in
Florida. He said he and his wife had spent the night
in Atlanta and he had seen my by-line in the paper.

"I served in World War Two with a man named
Lewis Grizzard," he said. "You wouldn't be his son,
would you?"

"My daddy was in World War Two," I said. "He
was from Snellville, Georgia, and he was in the infantry."

"That was him, then," said the man. I could sense
some excitement in his voice.

I told him the story, in brief. I told him how my

daddy had gone back to war in Korea and how he
started drinking when he came back and how he
never could straighten out his life. I told the man
my daddy was dead.

"I'm sorry to hear that," the man said. "Your
daddy was the best soldier I ever saw."

I should have gotten more. I should have told the
man to stay right where he was and that I would
meet him and we would talk about Daddy. But I
was young and I was sick and it didn't seem as
important to me at the time as it does now.

But the man did tell me a few things:

"I was with your dad in France," he began. "To
tell you the truth, I'm not surprised he had a drinking problem. I had one for a while, but thank God, I
got over mine.

"Me and your dad drank up France. It was the
only way you could get through another night.
Your dad was great with kids. That's why his platoon was always made up mostly of kids. They
would always go in first. They weren't as afraid as
the rest of us.

"Lewis didn't think he would make it back home.
He used to say, 'I don't guess I'll ever see Georgia or
my wife or my mother again.' He always thought
that sooner or later, he'd lead that first wave in, and
he'd get it.

"But I never saw a braver man. He pushed his
men, but he never asked them to do anything that
he wouldn't be out in front of. I could never understand how a man could be so tender, so kind, and
still be the fighting man that he was. I guess folks

like him were from the old school. He loved his
country. I was proud to have served with him."

I had never talked with anybody who was actually with my father in the war. I had heard all his
stories, and I knew that he had distinguished himself in combat, but I had never really put him there,
out front at the front.

A "fighting man" is how the caller had described
Daddy. I guess he killed some people. And I guess
he was scared. I couldn't imagine myself in the
same situation. Fighting by day, drinking by night
to chase away the anxiety of facing another battle,
another possibility of death.

Yet, my father—Daddy—had done it. "Never
saw a braver man," the caller said.

And what did that make me? I wondered.

Daddy wanted West Point for me. He talked
about it when I was barely old enough to understand what West Point was.

"I have this mahvelous friend who is in the Senate," Daddy would say. "He can get you an appointment to the Point."

After he and Mother divorced, Daddy still talked
about West Point with me. Perhaps if he and
Mother had stayed married, perhaps if I had grown
through adolescence in a military family, I would
have shared his desire that I go to West Point.

When I was fifteen, and Vietnam was still on the
back pages, I needed a physical examination to play
in a Babe Ruth League baseball tournament. There
was a new, young doctor in Grantville. My mother
took me there for the examination. The doctor al-

legedly charged smaller fees than the doctors in Newnan, the county seat.

The doctor listened to my heart. Then he listened some more. He said to my mother, "Has anyone ever told you your son has a heart murmur?"

I could see the expression of shock in my mother's face. There is something wrong with my son's heart?

"I really don't see any problem with it right now," the doctor said, "but it's something you probably should have checked occasionally."

I turned eighteen in the fall of 1964 when I was a freshman at the University of Georgia. Vietnam was sneaking up on the front pages by now. I registered for the draft. I never considered doing otherwise. Besides, I wasn't going to be drafted anyway. At least not for four years. I had my 2-S deferment and by the time I left college, I was certain the unpleasantness involving Vietnam would be long over.

There was some guilt. I was the son of a soldier, a brave, oft-decorated soldier. I developed a special feeling for the uniform early in my life, Daddy's uniform. My earliest memories of my father always have him in uniform. We were living in Columbus, Georgia, soon after Daddy's return from Korea. He was stationed at Fort Benning.

My parents were entertaining army friends at our new house one evening. I had been banished to my bedroom. I was five. I lay in the darkness of my room and listened to the laughter of my parents' party. The more I listened, the more I felt left out, abandoned. I listened until I could bear it no longer, and then ran from my bedroom toward the light in the den. As soon as I burst into the room and saw the disapproval on my mother's face, I leaped into the arms of my father. I knocked a drink from his hand. The liquid covered the front of his uniform shirt.

"I told you to stay in your room!" my mother shouted at me. "Look at your daddy's shirt!"

That uniform was so special. I didn't know why exactly, but men who wore that uniform commanded more of my childish esteem than those who didn't.

And I had soiled the uniform. I hid my face in my father's arms and began to sob.

"Young man," my mother began another verbal onslaught, "you have taken the rag off the bush."

(I never understood why my mother said I had taken the rag off the bush when I reached the limits of her patience, but I knew when I heard that phrase, I was perilously close to a thrashing.)

My mother spoke to my father.

"Take him back and I want you to wear him out."

I knew I had been the recipient of a giant break at that point. My mother was far superior to my father in handing out parental discipline.

Daddy led me to the bathroom. He closed the door behind us.

"I'm not going to whip you," he said, "but I don't want your mother to know it. When I hit my belt against the dirty clothes hamper, you holler."

The gods were beaming at me.

"Whap!" went my father's belt on the dirty clothes hamper.

"Waaaaa!" I screamed.

We probably would have been safe had Daddy and I not both become tickled.

Suddenly, my mother opened the door and there we stood laughing.

She smiled too. Then she wet a towel and began wiping Daddy's shirt clean. I went back to bed, comforted by the fact I had not soiled the uniform forever. The laughter started again soon afterward, and again I felt ostracized, but I remained in bed. I had already dodged one bullet. I didn't want to push my luck with a second.

As I grew older I still had enormous respect for the uniform. I was a Cub Scout. I wore the blue and gold. I was a Boy Scout. I wore the red and brown. My freshman year in college, they put me in air force ROTC. I went to see a man about getting my uniform.

"You need to get another physical, first," the man said.

I asked why.

"We checked your records, and you have some sort of heart problem."

I had forgotten all about that. The doctor had called it "a heart murmur," but he had allowed me to play ball anyway.

I had the physical. Now the doctors gave the problem a new name. They called it an "aortic insufficiency."

I never got the air force uniform. They waived me from the program because of my heart.

I told my mother.

"Your daddy did enough, son," she said. "You don't owe the service anything."

But I did. At least I thought I did. Actually, I felt it was my father whom I owed. He should have the thrill, I thought, to see me in my own uniform.

"Son," he would say, "you look absolutely mahvelous."

It was maybe six months after I was turned down for ROTC, Daddy turned up at my dorm room one day. I could not bear to look him in the eyes when I told him I was physically unfit for the service. He had gone through two years. He had worn the uniform, and, now, I was unfit for it.

I told him about the heart problem.

"In the name of God, son!" he said. "Is it serious?"

I told him I didn't think so, but the Air Force man wouldn't give me a uniform because of it.

"You won't have to be going in the service when you graduate, then?" he asked me.

I said I didn't think so.

"I was worried about that," he said. "Vietnam. I fought enough battles for both of us."

There was comfort in that. Still, I felt I had betrayed him in some way. Whatever that link is between father and son, it forgoes the feeling in the son that he must somehow emulate the father. That feeling said that somehow I had to prove my own courage, prove it to him. How could I be his son if I didn't show some of the mettle that surely had been passed down to me?

And perhaps I did show him there was no reluctance on my part to follow at least in some of his footsteps. Then he would know—and I would prove to myself once and for all—that he had not failed me, that no matter what happened afterwards, his heroic stance in combat would never be tarnished.

The point obviously was a moot one, however, because the service would not have me, regardless of the reasons I so badly wanted it. When I left school in 1968, I was reclassified by the draft board 1-Y. I understood that they would not call me until the enemy was marching up my street.

I told myself—I continue to tell myself—I would have gone if I had been able. I turned my anger against the war protestors. That was one way I dealt with my guilt, with my feelings of inadequacy. I never could rid myself of it completely.

If I couldn't fight while others my age were fighting, then how could I have known for certain if I had my daddy's guts? There is no sterner test of a man than war, I thought.

Danny Thompson was my best friend as a kid. We played in the same mudholes when we were seven. He didn't go to college. He got drafted.

I was home for a weekend visiting my mother. Danny stopped by the house. We went for a ride and stopped by the old baseball field. Danny played first. I pitched.

I asked him if he thought he would be sent to Vietnam.

"I guess I'll be there for a year," he said.

He could get killed, I thought to myself. Danny Thompson—God, we've been Cub Scouts together —could get killed in Vietnam. And here we sat by the old baseball field in Moreland, and we were old enough that they could send us to a war and we could get killed.

I asked him if he was afraid.

"A little," he said.

I was in awe of him. I felt sorry for him.

"You're lucky," Danny said.

"But I'll never know," I said.

"Know what?"

"If I could face it. If I could go and fight and not run, not cry."

"You could if you had to."

"My daddy did it."

"You probably could, too."

Danny made it back. Other friends didn't. I went to the Vietnam Veterans Memorial in Washington ten years after the war was over and found their names. I looked at other names on the wall, too. I was struck by the number of "Jr.'s" by the names. First-borns of other veterans, I concluded. I am a "Jr.," too. The guilt came back again, as it has to so many times in my life.

"You probably could, too," Danny had said.

But I'll never know. And the burden of not ever knowing always will be mine.

My daddy joined the army on June 6, 1942. On October 8, 1943, he arrived overseas. He was a first sergeant with Company K, the 110th Infantry.

Several years ago, I had gone through an old cedar chest at my mother's house. Inside were pictures of me when I was a child, scrapbooks, and the family Bible. I also found a folder that contained many of Daddy's military records.

I sat on the floor and carefully opened the folder. The first thing I came across was a carbon of a press release announcing that Daddy had been awarded the Bronze Star. Across the top of the first page was written, *Mama's copy.* Daddy had sent it home for his mother to see. She died only a few months afterward.

I knew very few details of Daddy's career. As I read the press release, I was struck soundly by this lack of knowledge.

I knew he had won the Bronze Star, but I had no idea of what he actually had done. The words, typed more than thirty years earlier, came storming off the page at me. Here was proof! Here was the greatness that was my father, written in official language. Here was a record I always could keep. This was not an actor in some combat movie. This was my daddy! There were words in praise of him and his courage and strength. This was before the fall. This was from whence I had sprung. Certainly I must have inherited some of this, and, had I been able, certainly I could have at least partially matched some of this. One generation later the strain that passed down such character certainly would have remained strong.

I read the release once. And then, I read it again. I felt the sense of a great archeological find. The Dead Sea Scrolls were in my hand. I knew this man who did these things. I knew how he smelled, how he talked, how it felt to be cradled in his arms. And, yet, I didn't know him. The daddy I had known for most of my life was a man in trouble, a man barely hanging on. A man who drank to forget, who gave me great disappointments, who wasn't there the times I needed him most.

But read this! Read this and know that my daddy —my daddy—no matter that he later failed at the accepted standards of manhood, he once by-God soared above them:

From: 28th Division PRO
 By—Sgt. J. J. Curtin
 Co. K 110th Inf.
 For Immediate Release

WITH THE 28TH INFANTRY DIVISION IN GERMANY, 20 March 1945—First Sergeant Lewis McD. Grizzard of Snellville, Georgia, has recently been awarded the Bronze Star medal by Major General Norman D. Cota, commanding general of the 28th "Keystone" Division, for "heroic action against the enemy" during the battle for Colmar in Alsace.

A member of Company K, 110th Infantry, Sgt. Grizzard distinguished himself on 6 February 1945 when the division joined other Seventh Army units in sealing the Colmar pocket, liberated the city of Colmar and then swept the remnants of the German defenders across the Rhine.

The enemy was holding the Rhine-Rhone River Canal outside the town of Rustenhart, France. They were dug in on both sides of the canal on high ground, supported by three concrete pill boxes and artillery. Company K, advancing on level ground toward the canal, without artillery or armored support, were greeted by stream after stream of devastating cross machine-gun fire and punishing artillery. Casualties were heavy, and after a grueling fire fight against such tremendous odds, the company was pinned down and forced to seek cover. Sgt. Grizzard, when notified of the wounding of all officers except one, quickly realized the seriousness of the situation. He moved forward to the aid of the lone remaining officer through a hail of machine-gun fire, while artillery and mortar shells tore up the ground around him. Exercising great skill and with utter disregard for his own safety, he moved about as an invaluable aid to the remaining officer, assisting him in maneuvering the company into a more advantageous position. Being a veteran soldier, he had tremendous steadying effect on the men of the company, who were almost to a man, green and fresh from training camps.

When the remaining officer went back in an attempt to obtain additional support for his company and make his report, Sgt. Grizzard took over the company. He personally directed the setting up of a defensive position outside the town of Rustenhart, thereby enabling our forces to hold the town until the necessary armor and artillery support arrived the following morning.

Sgt. Grizzard, who entered the Army on 6 June 1942, has been overseas since 8 October 1943. He was with the 28th during its drive through the Normandy hedgerows, Belgium, Luxembourg and finally into Germany where the division jabbed into the Siegfried Line—the first Allied unit to penetrate the Reich in strength. He also participated in the fierce fighting to stem the German thrust into Belgium and later took part in the Seventh Army "squeeze play" offensive on the Colmar, in which the "Keystone" Division took Colmar and pushed to the west bank of the Rhine.

He is the husband of Christine Grizzard of 1225 Princess Ave., Atlanta, Georgia, and has been awarded the Combat

Infantryman's Badge, the Purple Heart, and the Good Conduct Medal.

I continued searching through the folder. How could such material like this be left to yellow with age? Why hadn't my mother told me there was this marvelous (mahvelous) cache of information. Obviously, she had known the details of her husband's heroics. Why hadn't she shared them with me before? This removed all doubt about my father. This proved what I had hoped all along. He was a victim of circumstances, not weakness. God knows what combat could do to a man. My daddy could beat up anybody's daddy. Now, I knew it for certain.

I found a letter. It was dated February 10, 1945. The letter was from Daddy to Mother.

Dearest Wife:

I have a few minutes, so I will write you. I wish I could see you and I am certainly lonesome for you.

The fighting has been heavy, but I am okay. I think they have put me in for a medal. I will write more on that when I hear, but tell all the folks to watch the papers to see what is going on over here. I think this will be all over soon and I can be coming home to you.

I don't have time to send money home yet, but, darling, Joe is coming home (he was wounded), and when he calls you, he will have something for you. If he wants you to meet him some place in Tennessee or Kentucky go and see him and he will tell you everything that is going on here. He has $100 for you.

I haven't heard from you since December. Maybe before too much longer, I will hear. How's all the folks? Hope they are fine. How are the cousins? When I come home, honey, we will make up for lost time. Don't forget I love you, honey. Darling, it is for always. Stay sweet as you are.

Always,
Lewis

I dug deeper. There was a record of Daddy's battlefield commission to second lieutenant on April 18, 1945. There was the record of his Purple Heart, "for wounds received as a result of enemy action on 2 Aug. 1944."

There was a copy of a letter of commendation from Third Battalion Headquarters. It was dated 27 September 1945. Lt. Colonel Richard L. Jarvis had written the letter:

1. It is my desire at this time to highly commend 2nd Lt. Lewis McD. Grizzard 0-2008593, for his continuous, outstanding work since joining this Battalion.

2. Lt. Grizzard's outstanding leadership has been in evidence since he joined this Battalion as a private. His steady and continuous rise through all the enlisted grades and finally to a battlefield promotion to the grade of 2nd Lt., are evidence of the high qualities of leadership in this officer.

3. Lt. Grizzard's ability to command this respect and devotion of his men, his highly developed sense of humor, his ability to become outstanding in whatever position he occupies, and his ability to make friends quickly and easily among any group of strangers, all make it possible for me to unhesitatingly recommend Lt. Grizzard for any position for which his grade and experience qualify him.

4. I would be extremely well pleased to have Lt. Grizzard serve under me either in combat or in garrison duties.

I also found Daddy's honorable discharge. It was granted 18 April 1945 in order that he be able to accept his battlefield commission.

I also found his certificate of military service. It noted the prior active service from 6 June 1942 until the honorable discharge in 1945.

It then noted the second service from 19 April 1945 until 1 April 1953. His last grade was captain. The certificate said that Daddy's second discharge was "other than honorable."

I asked my mother why she had not told me of these records.

"Son," she said, "it's been so long, I didn't even know I still had them. So much of his things got lost after we separated."

"He didn't get any military benefits after he left the army, did he?"

"As far as I know," said my mother, "not a one."

"But how could they do that to him? How could they not recognize his previous honorable discharge and the Bronze Star, and the time in Korea? My God, the man gave the army the best part of his life!"

"Son, when he came back from Korea, he just wasn't the same anymore. There were times I really didn't know him. He had something inside him that was eating him up. He wouldn't tell me what it was. He wouldn't tell anybody. He couldn't sleep. He'd have nightmares. He'd call people long distance at night and cry over the phone.

"But I want you to know something, and I want you never to forget it. Your daddy was a good soldier. He fought for his country. And he never complained about it, even at the end when the army said he was unfit for service. He never blamed the army. He never blamed his country."

"Was it mostly the drinking that caused him to get kicked out?"

"Mostly that, but you shouldn't remember him as a failure. War killed your daddy more than anything else."

I suddenly remembered something. I remembered that after Daddy came home from Korea and we were living in Columbus while he was stationed at Benning, he and my mother had separate bedrooms.

I asked her why.

"He was not the same man when he came home" is what she said.

CHAPTER
5

DADDY CAME HOME FROM WORLD WAR II IN OCTOBER 1945.
I was born in October 1946. The other original Baby
Boomers and I are all turning forty this year.

Daddy was stationed in Fort Benning, one hundred miles south of Atlanta. My mother had moved
back in with Una in Atlanta during the war. Jobs
were hard to come by, and my mother initially did
not want to give up her job and move down to
Benning.

Daddy took up residence at the Bachelor Officers'
Quarters (BOQ) and took the *Man O' War* passenger train from Columbus to Atlanta each weekend
to visit my mother.

My mother's sister Una was also married to a returning soldier. His name was Stokes. Stokes had
moved in with his wife and they shared the second
bedroom in my mother's apartment.

Stokes was out of the army and refused to seek

employment. One weekend, my father had a long discussion with Stokes and convinced him he should look for a job. A couple of days later, Stokes announced he would, in fact, seek work. That was forty years ago. My Uncle Stokes hasn't been heard from since.

As my mother tells it, Daddy quickly became fed up with his weekend wife and instructed her to move to Fort Benning or look for another husband.

Mother thought it over, she remembers, for about three seconds before she decided to quit her job and move in with him. My brokenhearted Aunt Una moved in, too.

I was a preemie. I wasn't supposed to arrive until late November. I arrived October 20. I weighed only five pounds.

"I was certain something was wrong with you," my Aunt Una would tell me later. "You were tiny and you had the reddest little face. I told Jesse [another sister], 'There's something wrong with Christine's baby.'"

They say my daddy spoiled me from the very first day. He was an athletic officer at Benning when I was born.

"You weren't three weeks old, and he had you on his lap while he was coaching a basketball game," my mother has said, laughing now.

"He would walk around the post with you in his arms and stop everybody he saw to show them his son. He even took you with us to an Officer's Club dance soon after I got out of the hospital.

"When the band took a break, everybody wanted Lewis to play the piano and sing. He wouldn't even let me hold you while he performed. He put you on his lap and played right along. You seemed to be enjoying yourself."

My earliest memories go back to a vague remembrance that has to do with the two years we spent in Camp Chaffee, Arkansas, where Daddy was reassigned in 1948, shortly before I turned two.

I have a notion of our house there. There was a front porch, and I backed off it on my tricycle one day. There was a place Daddy enjoyed eating called The Smorgasbord. I wouldn't pronounce it. I would say, "Daddy, let's go to the 'smagusbod,' " and he understood, and he would take us.

I remember my mother getting sick. And then I remember my Aunt Una coming to live with us again. She was there to take care of me after they put my mother in the hospital.

I didn't realize it at the time, of course, but my mother nearly died. She had a scalp infection that somehow got worse. Her hair fell out. My Aunt Una once said that her mother, my grandmother, always worried about her girl child, Christine, because she had been born with the "veil." There was a belief that if the placenta stayed on the baby's head it was a portent of disasters that would later befall the baby.

Mother became critical. Doctors decided the one chance she had was to be found at Walter Reed Hospital in Washington.

"It was the first time I had ever flown," my mother would remember later. "I was frightened to death. I was frightened the plane might crash and I'd never see you or your daddy again. Once the plane finally made it to Washington, I knew I had a chance to live."

Nobody else was certain, however. Doctors called Daddy soon after Mother arrived at Walter Reed and advised him he had best get to Washington as soon as possible, that Mother could die at any time.

We took an all-night train. The memory of that trip is quite vivid.

We had a sleeper, a roomette with one bed. I was nearly four by now. I remember how peaceful it seemed in that bed with my father as the train rocked eastbound through the night. Daddy told me stories, and we laughed together. Late in the evening, I decided I was hungry.

"In the name of God," he said, "what do you want to eat at this hour?"

I said I wanted a ham sandwich and chocolate milk.

Daddy rang the porter. When he came to the room, Daddy said, "Is there any way under the sun you can get this starving child a ham sandwich and some chocolate milk?"

"The dining car's been closed two hours," said the porter.

"I'm hungry, Daddy," I added to the problem.

"I can't let him go to sleep hungry," Daddy said.

The porter was gone a half hour. Finally, he returned. With the ham sandwich. With the chocolate milk.

"I slipped in the kitchen and got the food," said the porter.

"How much do I owe you?" Daddy asked.

"Not a thing," said the porter. "I got a boy at

home 'bout his age. I know all 'bout boys gettin' hungry late at night."

Daddy laughed and shook the porter's hand. I ate my sandwich and drank my chocolate milk, and then I went to sleep with my arms around my daddy's neck.

Mother got well. They said it was a miracle. Daddy was able to get restationed at Fort Myer, Virginia, just outside Washington. Aunt Una stayed with us, even after Mother got out of the hospital. I bragged I had two mothers, and I thought I did.

We were in Fort Myer nine months. We lived in married housing. Aunt Una got a job at the Pentagon and met a new man, and they dated. My daddy taught me to say all sorts of clever things when the man—to be my future Uncle John—came over to pick up Aunt Una.

He taught me to say "bullshit." He thought that was funny. I thought it was funny. Even Una's man, John, thought it was funny. My mother was appalled. Aunt Una was embarrassed.

"Next time John comes to pick up your Aunt Una," Daddy said to me, "and he asks if she's ready, you say, 'Not right now, she's washing her avoirdupois.'"

Avoirdupois, the abdominal region, was not that easy for a four-year-old, but I practiced with Daddy until I had perfected it.

The next time John came over he fell right into the trap.

"Your Aunt Una ready?" he asked me.

"Not right now," I said. "She's washing her avoirdupois."

Daddy and John laughed. My mother didn't.

"Did you teach him to say that word?" my mother, who wasn't sure what it meant, only that it sounded risqué, asked Daddy.

"I don't know where he picks up things like that," Daddy answered, laughing.

I sensed how cute I must be, and I began shouting "avoirdupois" at the top of my lungs.

"You don't even know what an avoirdupois is," my mother said.

"I know Aunt Una's got a clean one," I said.

Daddy fell on the couch and rolled with laughter. Aunt Una walked out, ready for her date.

"Aunt Una!" I shouted. "Get your avoirdupois cleaned up?"

"What did you say?" Una asked.

"Lewis has been teaching him dirty words again," said my mother.

Una and John left for their date. My mother lectured my father. I sat and listened, confident my first performance as a comedian had been a successful one.

We were happy there. When Mother had recovered, she took me on long walks. Often, we strolled through Arlington cemetery. And we would go over to see the changing of the guard at the Tomb of the Unknown Soldier. We drove along the Potomac, sometimes, just the three of us. We went for picnics in the Shenandoah Mountains, we ate at Hot Shoppes, and Daddy took me to see the Senators play.

I was Daddy's boy. When we drove I kneeled on the backseat and put my arms around him. I rode

on his back. He pushed me in this little car I got for
Christmas. He told me stories about when he was a
kid. He told me about Lucille Wellmaker and Hester
Camp and I would want to hear the stories again
and again.

He had pet names for me. He called me "Ponder."
He would say, "Look a-yonder, Ponder." He called
me "Mr. Sabeera." I have no idea where that name
came from, but when supper was ready, he would
come to the front door and call out to me in the
yard, "Mr. Sa-beeeee-rah, it's time to eat."

I never remember being left with a baby-sitter. I
went where my parents went. I became a regular at
the Officers' Club at Fort Myer, as I had been at
Benning.

Mother and Daddy had their song. It was "The
Tennessee Waltz." They would leave me at the table to dance, and I would watch them. I thought
dancing was a little silly, but I at least gave them
one dance to themselves.

Daddy could play and sing "The Tennessee
Waltz." He taught me to sing with him:

> *I was dancing*
> *With my darling,*
> *The night they were playin'*
> *The beautiful Tennessee Waltz.*

Hearing that song, singing it with my daddy, or
watching my parents dance to it, made me happy. It
was their song, but it was our song, too, the
family's.

A child senses, I think, whether or not his or her parents share a deep love. I think mine had that, at least at some point.

I know Mother loved Daddy.

"You know what he used to do?" she would tell me as I was growing up. "He would never come home at night from work without bringing me some kind of present. Sometimes, it wouldn't be much. Maybe a bar of candy or a stick of gum.

"But sometimes it would be flowers or perfume, or even clothes. He had the best taste in women's clothes. I rarely shopped without him. I would try on something and ask him how it looked.

"He'd say, 'In the name of God, Christine, get that awful garment off!' Or, if he liked what I was trying out, he would say, 'You look mahvelous, Christine! Buy it quickly before somebody else does.'

"He was so amusing. All the other wives—and Una, too—absolutely loved him. He was always so polite, always so flattering. I didn't think I could give him up. But I had no choice."

And he loved her.

She wanted a house after I was born at Fort Benning. Daddy got her one. She wanted a sewing machine. Daddy got her one of those, too. And one night a man came to our house selling vacuum cleaners, the rage for housewives.

The salesman was a bit squirrely, and Daddy thought he was a riot.

"Show me that mahvelous trick again," he'd say, "where you balance the ball at the end of one of those air hoses."

"Christine," he said. "Would you like to have one of these amazing devices?"

"I don't think we can afford it," said Mother, always the economist.

"In the name of God, woman," he bellowed, "I never want to see a broom in your hands again."

Turning to the salesman, he said, "Young man, you are a brilliant salesman. We'll take it!"

Mother and Daddy did practically everything together. They were great bridge players. Daddy would round up another couple from somewhere and then bring them to our house for a game.

I was never one to go quietly to my bedroom when there were festivities in another part of the house, as I mentioned. I usually spent the bridge games sleeping under the card table, against the players' legs and feet.

Mother was at all of Daddy's ball games. He insisted. Mother was what was known as a high-strung woman, which meant, in those days, she often would voice strong opinions about matters, sometimes to Daddy at rather high decibel levels.

"What used to make me so mad at him," Mother would laugh, "is he wouldn't argue with me. I don't care what I said, he'd just put his arms around me and pat the back of my head and say, 'Christine, Christine. Just hush and everything's going to be just fine.'"

When I would visit Daddy after he and Mother had separated, he always asked about her first. Again, a child senses things. I sensed how much he missed her. The demon that hounded him and cost him his wife must have had a powerful hold on him. Otherwise, he never could have given her up.

Often, I still see them together in my dreams. Daddy is young and he is laughing, and Mother has that long black hair, and they are dancing again to "The Tennessee Waltz." They are in love.

And when on occasion, I hear that song today, it stirs an old feeing in me that is left over from my earliest childhood. I thought that we—the three of us—would be singing that song together forever.

Included in that folder I had found at my mother's house were a number of Daddy's records from Korea. I found a copy of the orders that ended our stay at Fort Myer and that, for all practical purposes, ended the time we would spend together as a family.

The orders were dated 6 September 1950. I was just over a month from my fourth birthday. The orders read:

Subject: Travel Orders
To: Officers Involved
   Each of the following named officers is relieved from assignment and duty, station indicated, and is assigned to Far East Command, Yokohama, Japan, Shipment OM-W135-EF(a). Will proceed to Camp Stoneman Personnel Center, Pittsburgh, California, and report no later than 30 September 1950, for transportation via military aircraft or surface vessel.

One of the three officers named was 1st Lt. Lewis McD. Grizzard of South Post, Fort Myer, Virginia.

Daddy would say this later. He would say it often:

"The first time a man goes to war, he is not that afraid because he has no idea what he is getting into. The second time he goes to war, he is petrified. He knows what awaits him."

We moved out of Fort Myer shortly after Daddy received his new orders. We moved back to my mother's parents' house in Moreland. We would stay there while Daddy was gone. We had driven south in our Packard. Daddy was notorious for his slow driving.

"Can't you go any faster?" Mother would ask him, as we crept through the Carolinas.

"In the name of God, woman!" Daddy would reply. "This isn't Indianapolis!"

I was in the backseat with a baseball Daddy had given me. At some point during our trip, I decided to throw my ball out of the window. As soon as I let it go, I realized I had made a terrible mistake.

"What do you think you are doing, young man?" was Mother's initial response.

I would have explained I didn't know what had happened, that I simply had this sudden, overwhelming urge to throw my ball out the window just to see what a ball would do when thrown out of a Packard going thirty-eight miles an hour. The reason I didn't say that was because I wasn't even four years old yet and had not learned to make clever excuses. What I did was cry.

Daddy stopped the car, turned around and drove back down the road in search of my ball.

"You've spoiled this child," Mother said to Daddy.

"I don't have much time left with him, Christine," he replied. "Let me spoil him while I have the chance."

I really didn't understand the situation. Daddy said he was going away, but that he would be back. Mother said we were going to live with Mama Willie and Daddy Bun while Daddy was away and that I would enjoy living with them. I took her word for it.

We drove the Packard to Atlanta on September 19, 1950, to put Daddy on a train west. We sent him away to war again with a shoe box filled with fried chicken and biscuits. Mama Willie went with us. Before he stepped on the train, Daddy picked me up in his arms and squeezed me firmly. It was a once-in-a-lifetime squeeze. I haven't forgotten it.

Mother cried. So did Mama Willie. Daddy said he would write whenever he could.

"Be a good soldier," was the last thing he said to me.

I slept with my mother that night. We said a prayer for Daddy before we went to sleep. My mother's voice broke as she prayed. That was unsettling to me. A child can sense fear or dismay in a parent as easily as he or she can sense anger or love.

Mama Willie, a stout, strong woman with a firm, unwavering hand when it came to disciplinary matters, worked nights as a nurse. Daddy Bun farmed his twelve acres in Moreland and helped out at the tiny Atlanta & West Point depot. Wherever he went, I normally followed.

He was a tall, rawboned sort of a man, I think my mother got her shoulders from him. He had hollow cheeks and an air of seriousness about him that would easily disappear into a broad smile and a twinkle or two in his eyes.

He drank his coffee out of his saucer. I did that, too, for years until somebody told me it wasn't polite. I remember being at the breakfast table with him, and when he brought the saucer to his mouth for a slurp, his biceps would bulge. If he had been a football player, I like to think he would have been a defensive back who delivered jarring tackles to wide receivers who dared appear in his coverage area.

He had little or no formal education, but he built the best rabbit traps around. One eye was gone because of cataracts, but tell that to the squirrels he shot for dinner with his .22 rifle.

He was a master carpenter. And a bricklayer. He could hit a baseball all the way from the front yard, over into Mr. Cates' peach orchard. He taught me how to spread guano, how to catch a fish, and how to put apples in a homemade cider press.

He also helped further my lifelong fascination with trains. Daddy Bun even managed us a ride in the engine one day from Moreland to Newnan, the county seat, seven miles north. The engineer allowed me to blow the horn.

"Want to be an engineer when you grow up?" he asked me.

"No," I said, "I want to be a soldier like my daddy."

A train took my daddy away. One, I was certain, would bring him back.

Each time a train stopped in Moreland, I asked my grandfather, "Is my daddy on this train?"

"No," he would say, "but he'll be back before you know it."

My grandparents didn't have a television. Daddy Bun and I spent the evenings in a swing on their porch. He told good stories, too. I snuggled close to him. There were always a lot of dogs around to pet, and Daddy Bun took me for rides on his back, like Daddy did.

One day, somebody stole the Packard. Just walked into the driveway, got into the Packard, and drove away.

My mother was hysterical. Daddy Bun got his shotgun and drove off in his truck to find the person who stole our Packard. He wasn't gone very long.

"I found the Packard," he said to Mother.

"Who stole it?" she asked.

"One of them Porter boys," Daddy Bun answered. "They're not quite right. They marry their cousins."

Mother rode away with Daddy Bun and in a few minutes, she was back driving the Packard.

I was fascinated by my first involvement with crime.

"Did you have to shoot anybody, Daddy Bun?" I asked my grandfather.

"No," he said, "but you never know what's going to happen when you deal with a Porter."

Living with my grandparents was a totally new

experience. Mama Willie was a stern disciplinarian, dedicated to purging my spoiled personality while she had the chance.

When she spanked me, she did it in earnest. I was used to Daddy pulling his punches. One of my cousins told me Mama Willie's middle name was Ruby. She was attempting to exorcise some of my meanness out one day—I had taken a large spoon to her cake batter—and when I had heard all I wanted to hear, I said, "Aw, Ruby, why don't you just be quiet?"

She attacked in a split second, flailing at my hindparts with both hands. I desperately tried to block her blows.

"Don't you never sass me!" she said.

I was in tears by then.

My grandfather walked in from the field just in time to save me.

"Don't be too rough on him," he said to my grandmother. "A boy's liable to act any way when he misses his daddy."

I didn't really understand my grandfather's logic there, but I didn't care. He had snatched me from the jaws of a sound thrashing.

The old records show Daddy joining Company M of the 8th Regiment of the 1st Cavalry, 23 October 1950. I had celebrated my fourth birthday three days earlier. Before I sat down to write this book, I asked my mother if she remembered what we did on my fourth birthday in 1950.

"Mama Willie baked you a pound cake," she remembered, and I was surprised that she could.

"And we didn't know where Daddy was?"

"We didn't know anything," she said.

I've heard this story before. I've written it in other books. Forgive if I repeat here, but I must. Just once more:

IPSOK *Korea, 2 Nov. 1950 (UPI)—Chinese Communist hordes, attacking on horse and on foot to the sound of bugle calls, cut up Americans and South Koreans at Unsan today in an Indian-style massacre that may prove to be the costliest of the Korean War.*

Two combat regiments were badly chewed up and hundreds of civilians—men, women, and children—who tried to escape along the roads leading from Unsan were killed by enemy machine-gun and mortar fire.

The Communists charged in the frosty early morning hours in an attack so vicious, it left the surprised and confused Americans no choice but to run. Many did not escape.

Here, in the words of some men lucky enough to escape, is the story of how the Chinese infiltrated the lines of the United States First Cavalry Division and the South Korean First Division:

PFC Joseph Sutherland of North Gardens, Virginia, said: "I woke up when they started shooting the fellows in the foxholes around me. I couldn't see anything until a tank came along. I climbed on and fell off three times, or was pulled off by others trying to get on. Then, the tank burst into flames and we all started running."

PFC Henry Tapper of High Point, North Carolina, said: "Someone woke me up and asked if I could hear a bunch of horses on the gallop. I couldn't hear anything. The bugles started playing taps, but far away. Someone blew a whistle and our area was shot to hell in a matter of minutes. I'm not too sure how it all happened right now, but I knew we lost more of our outfit there than got out."

"There was no such thing as fighting back," Lt. Patrick J. McDonald of Vancouver, Washington, said. "The chances were greatest that you would hit one of your own men than one of the enemy. . . ."

Daddy's story. I know it by heart. "Late the night before, we had set up camp. We were right by a rice paddy. It was cold. God, was it cold. I remember that as platoon leader, I had had to ask all my men to fill out a form telling their religious affiliation. I had a couple men put down atheist.

"Early the nest morning, it looked like that rice paddy just got up and started shooting. I'd fought through Belgium and Luxembourg and France during World War II, but that was different. The German soldiers were like us. The Germans didn't want to die any more than we did. We could count on what the Krauts would do.

"But the Gooks were different. MacArthur had said they weren't coming into the war, but that morning, they were sure as hell in it.

"They were crazy. I always figured they were hopped up on dope. You'd kill one and then more would take his place. They attacked in waves. Some of them were on horses. Firecrackers were going off in the sky, and they were rattling pots and pans, it seemed, and bugles were playing. They didn't care if they died. They just swooped down on us before we knew it.

"The other officers were falling all over the place. I got some men, and we dug in. We were sort of in this box foxhole. There must have been thirty of us in there. We took a direct mortar hit, and that wiped out a lot of us. We had a chaplain with us. A kid went crazy and jumped out of the hole, screaming. Machine-gun fire hit him instantly and took his head off clean as a whistle. The head rolled back in the hole. I'll never forget that kid's face. There was a big smile on it.

"The chaplain said to me, 'You've just seen a man go to heaven.' Those two that said they were atheists were in the hole with us. You know what they say, that there are no atheists in a foxhole? That's right. Those two were praying as hard and loud as any of us. They were begging the chaplain to get God to forgive them.

"Men just started running. There was no order to retreat. We were completely overrun. There were dead all around me in the hole. I knew I had only one chance. I played like I was dead. I had been hit in the hip and there was blood all over the bottom of my pants.

"The Chinese were pulling us out of the hole. They pulled me out. I tried not to breathe. They stacked me in a pile with other dead GIs. I didn't move. I was scared to death.

"A group of Chinese had been standing near where I lay. After maybe thirty minutes, they wandered off somewhere. I rolled behind a rock. Suddenly I saw another American coming toward me, crawling. We didn't speak. We both hid behind the rock until we decided it was safe to move out.

"We had no idea where we were going. He was a private. I said, 'Let's run,' and we lit out."

What is left of the story came from another piece of paper I found in the packet of my father's records. It was a clip from the *Atlanta Constitution* dated November 20, 1950:

GOD BLESS THAT CHINESE COMMUNIST

That was the rare benediction Sunday night from a Moreland, Georgia, army wife.

It came through her tears when she learned a chubby little Chinese soldier, sorry he had wounded her husband and another American, nursed the two Infantrymen back to health and escorted them to the United Nations lines.

Mrs. Lewis Grizzard told The Constitution *Chinese Communist or not, the enemy soldier must have been "a good man to do that for my husband and the other boy."*

The Constitution *informed Mrs. Grizzard of the Red soldier's change of heart after International News Service correspondent Lee Ferrero told the story in a dispatch from the Northwest Korea Front. Ferrero's dispatch said the Communist soldier, identified as Pvt. Chan, surrendered to a First Cavalry patrol Sunday after acting as a guide and nurse for Lt. Lewis Grizzard and Pvt. Henry Hause of Lancaster, Massachusetts, for two weeks.*

The elated Mrs. Grizzard, who cried because "I am so happy," said she would have a restful sleep Sunday "for the first time in six weeks." She said she had not heard from her husband in that time.

Grizzard and Hause were wounded in the bloody Nov. 2 surprise rout of the First Cavalry's 8th Regiment. And Mrs. Grizzard said she has been "worried to death" since then because she knew her husband was in the 8th Regiment.

The two Americans, Ferrero wrote, told of a harrowing story of hiding out in enemy territory for sixteen days after their battalion was cut off.

The unit was ordered back to the United Nations lines as best it could after a rescue attempt met with such ferocity that to have continued the mission would have been suicidal.

Grizzard and Hause, after two days, saw a single enemy soldier approaching them from a nearby hill. Grizzard said:

"We had a .45 and we figured the two of us certainly could handle one unarmed soldier, but he suddenly hurled a grenade at us."

Both Americans were wounded by the grenade and expected the coup de grace at any moment, when the enemy soldier came up to them. Then came a pleasant surprise, Hause said:

"I was stunned to find the Chinese soldier treating my wound. Then, he apparently wanted to help us when he found we were Americans."

Then, for fourteen days, the Americans and the Chinese straggler ate and slept the best they could until they stumbled into a First Cavalry patrol Sunday.

The two Americans said they owed their lives to "Chan the Chink," and they spoke his name with affection.

Grizzard told how the Red soldier had even dickered for food for them with North Koreans and had once paid for two sweet potatoes out of his own pocket.

Chan worked his way slowly toward American lines, at times bluffing his way past North Korean soldiers while trying to find the route.

During his forays, the Americans were hidden in huts with the cooperation of sympathetic Korean farmers. Both men were in bad shape from exposure and the recent cold blast.

It was the first time a Chinese soldier had accompanied surviving Americans to safety and it tended to substantiate reports of other wounded Americans that the Chinese do not want to *fight Americans, INS correspondent Ferrero said. In all such reported cases, the Chinese were former Nationalist soldiers pressed into service by the Chinese Communists.*

Maj. Gen. Hobart R. Gay of the First Cavalry Division was so happy to hear of Chan's friendliness, he offered him a job—"if he can cook."

Whether or not he can cook, Chan was the most popular Chinese Red on the Northwest Front Sunday night. And Mrs. Grizzard seconds that motion.

Lt. Grizzard . . . won a battlefield commission promotion to second lieutenant in the European Theater.

The couple has a four-year-old son, Lewis, Jr.

I was in my grandparents' yard in Moreland playing with my uncle's two birddogs, Sam and Duke. Birddogs are great with kids. Sam and Duke were in the process of licking me in the face. It was only later in life that people develop an aversion to being licked in the face by dogs.

Mother walked down the concrete steps that led from the kitchen. She asked me to sit down next to her in the chairs that sat under the big willow tree. It was under that tree and in those chairs I had sat with my grandfather while he told me stories about old dogs he used to have and what made things grow.

Mother had been crying. I could see that.

"Your daddy is missing in action in Korea," she said to me.

I didn't know what that meant. Mother went on to explain.

"He was in a battle and the army doesn't know where he is right now, but that doesn't mean that anything bad has happened to him. He's just, uh, missing."

I believed her. But I don't know if she believed herself. The next few weeks must have been hell for her. As a child I had it easy. I knew from Mother's tears at night, from how she seemed to cling closer to me, something was not exactly right, but a child can cope when there are birddogs to lick him in the face and a grandfather to tell him stories.

We prayed together each night after turning out the light. We prayed Daddy was safe.

We mentioned him in our prayers before meals. My grandfather, who described himself as a "foot-washing Baptist," always said the blessing.

"Lord," he would say, "please watch over our loved one and bring him back to us safely."

The preacher at the Methodist Church mentioned Daddy, too.

"And, please, Father, bring Lieutenant Grizzard back home to his wife and child."

I asked my mother, "Will praying help Daddy come back?"

"It's all we can do," she answered.

Alone, or with Sam and Duke, I began to pray on my own. I made certain I prayed with my eyes closed. My grandmother told me God doesn't listen when you pray with your eyes open.

Daddy's service record indicates he was a prisoner of war from November 5 until November 21, 1950. It was a couple of days after Chan returned him and Private Hause to the UN lines that the International News Service story hit the wires and the *Constitution* contacted Mother and told her Daddy was safe. She cried. My grandparents cried. I cried. We prayed some more. The preacher announced the wonderful news from his pulpit and after church several old ladies picked me up and kissed me and said, "I know you'll be glad to get your daddy back."

Certainly, I would. At the moment, however, I was quite interested in leaving the church so old ladies would stop picking me up and kissing me.

Daddy was first evacuated to a field hospital. Then he was transported to Japan, then on to Hawaii. He was to call us from there on Christmas Eve as he prepared to fly Christmas Day to San Francisco, his last stop before coming home.

The family gathered for the call at Uncle Grover and Aunt Jessie's house on the other side of the Atlanta and West Point railroad tracks, the reason being that Uncle Grover and Aunt Jessie had the only telephone in the family. There was some elation, I recall, to the fact the army was paying for the call and Daddy wouldn't have to phone collect.

I vaguely remember the conversation I had with him when the call finally came through. Mother was to talk first, of course. She started crying again. My grandmother was next. My grandfather was never one to talk much on the telephone, so he passed up his turn to Aunt Jessie.

Mother got back on the line and then she turned to me and said, "Come talk to your daddy."

I wasn't much into telephones myself at four, but I sat in Mother's lap and I was fine until Daddy started crying on the other end.

Everybody else stayed up late that night. They put me to bed. I slept. Santa came. My mother says she isn't sure what he brought me, but she thinks it was a cap pistol and another tricycle.

Daddy was in a hospital in San Francisco for a couple more weeks. His feet had suffered severe frostbite while Chan hid him and Hause from the enemy during the cruel Korean winter of 1950. He also suffered from malnutrition. The rice and potatoes Chan was able to scrounge for them had kept Daddy alive, but that was the extent of it.

He came home on January 11, 1951. The official greeting party at the Atlanta airport was Mother and me, Mama Willie and Daddy's sister, Rufy. There was hugging and kissing and more crying. An Atlanta reporter and photographer were there, too. I found the clipping of the story and photograph in the folder. Daddy is sitting on the left in the photograph. My mother, who was wearing a hat, smiled down on us from the center. Mama Willie, who also wore a hat, is on the right. I am sitting in Daddy's lap, and he is looking at me smiling. I am smiling back at him.

The caption under the photograph reads, "Lewis, Jr., Welcomes His Dad, Capt. Lewis Grizzard, Home from Korea."

The article with the photograph quoted Daddy as saying Korea could be won. "Nobody," he said, "can beat the American soldier."

When we returned to Moreland, an hour's drive from the Atlanta airport, the family gathered at Uncle Grover and Aunt Jessie's again, the reason this time being that they were the only members of the family—and one of the few in Moreland—to have a television.

John Cameron Swayze appeared with the news. Halfway through the newscast, a still photograph of Daddy's homecoming came on the screen and John Cameron Swayze told the nation, in the briefest of terms, how the Communist Chinese soldier had saved Daddy. I was too young to be impressed by my picture having been shown on national television.

The family wanted Daddy's story—his official version, of course. I would hear him tell it often—there were many versions; each time he told it, he told it differently—and each time, I envisioned the experience in my mind. I still do that.

Only now, it seems more of a nightmare. Before, Daddy was a hero in a grand adventure.

"Me and Private Hause started running. We were cold and hungry. And scared. I tried to act like I knew what I was doing to keep Hause from panicking. If he had known how close I was to losing it, I don't know what he would have done. I just told him, 'Be alert, soldier. We'll get out of this somehow.'

"It was cold. God knows, it was cold. We wandered over a small hill. All of a sudden, I looked down at the bottom and there was a soldier. I had a .45 strapped on and we had him outnumbered two to one. I reached for my weapon, but before I could get it out to fire, the soldier suddenly threw a grenade at us.

"It knocked both of us cold for a few seconds, I guess. We both had shrapnel wounds. My neck and hands were bleeding. He started coming toward us and I figured he was going to try to finish us.

"But the first thing he did was to wipe away the blood on my hands and then he pulled out some kind of bandage and wrapped my hands in it.

"We couldn't understand what he was saying, and he couldn't understand us. But after he checked our wounds, he motioned for us to follow him. All we could figure was that he was AWOL from the Reds and when he saw us, we frightened him and he threw the grenade. Then after he saw we were Americans, he wanted to take care of us so maybe we could lead him to our lines so he could give himself up and be safe.

"He first took us to a hut where an old Papa-San lived. The old man gave us some rice and some water. Chan and the old man talked to each other and I guess they were talking about what to do with us. There were enemy patrols all around, I figured, and I guess they did, too, and didn't think it was safe for us in the hut.

"Chan motioned again for us to follow him. It was dark out by now, but the moon was bright and I'll never forget how that Korean sky looked. It looked so close, like you could reach out and touch the stars.

"We followed Chan to a cave—a hole—in the side of one of the hills. He motioned for us to get inside the cave. We didn't have a better idea, so we crawled in. He gave us some straw to put over us to keep us as warm as possible, but it didn't do much good. There was barely room to stretch out in the cave.

"I curled up as tightly as I could and put the straw over me. I slept with my helmet on. It kept my head a little warm. I'd never known cold like Korea. I couldn't imagine how the place could ever thaw out.

"I slept a little and then I'd wake up for a while and shiver. I heard voices a couple of times when I was awake. They sounded very close. They were enemy soldiers, I'm sure. I remember having this crazy thought that if we surrendered to them, we could get warm. I was so cold that I was almost on the point of being able to accept death, just to get away from the cold.

"I didn't know how long we stayed in that hole. We could tell day from night. Chan had covered the entrance with straw, but light would seep in.

"He kept bringing us rice and one day he even brought us two sweet potatoes. We could even hear him dickering with North Korean soldiers to get food. They were that close to us at times.

"I really didn't think I would live through it all. I thought the cold would get me if the enemy didn't. I knew something was wrong with my feet. They had swollen. My boots got tighter and tighter. I would daydream about soaking my feet in a tub of hot water.

"I would close my eyes and picture Christine and my son. I once even thought of trying to tell Chan to bring me a pencil and some paper, so I could write them a message and maybe the Red Cross would find my body and they would send it home.

"But it wouldn't have done me any good to have

the paper or the pencil. My hands were too cold to hold a pencil, much less write with it.

"The smell got worse and worse in the cave. We had to crap and pee right in our pants. I could feel myself getting rawer and rawer. Chan got sick of the smell, too. He began handing us our food from the outside, rather than coming into the cave. I didn't blame him for that.

"I suppose he waited until he thought it was safe for us to move on, and then he came one day to the cave and motioned us out. Neither one of us were able to stand right away. Every inch of my body ached. I would try to stand, and then I would fall back down again. Hause finally got up, but Chan had to hold me up when we first started moving. My feet were like walking on two basketballs. Every step was pure torture. I don't know how far we walked, for how long. I still couldn't walk without Chan's help. He was a little fellow. I don't know how he had the strength to hold me up as long as he did.

"We finally came to another hut. I dropped to the ground and Chan went inside. He came back out and pulled me inside the hut. There was an old farmer and his wife inside. They gave us more rice and water. They had a fire, and I wanted to jump into the thing. The old man and woman didn't seem to want to come close to us. At first I thought they were afraid of us. Then I caught another smell of us, and didn't blame them for being standoffish.

"Chan let us rest by the fire for about a half hour after we ate, and then he motioned we had to go.

Getting on my feet again and leaving the fire was one of the hardest things I've ever had to do.

"We went back outside. It was still daylight, but I had no idea of the time. All of a sudden we heard voices. But this time the voices were speaking English. I can't describe the feeling I had. I was afraid I was dreaming again.

"But I looked down the road and I saw an American patrol coming toward us. 'God, don't let this be a mirage,' I said.

"When they came closer, Chan put me down on the ground and he saluted the soldiers. I was afraid they were going to do something to Chan, but all I could get out of my mouth was, 'He saved us. He saved us.'

"When we got back to the lines, and I told them what Chan had done, everybody patted him on his back and he smiled and smiled. They put him to work as a cook.

"We were transferred to a field hospital. We must have been an awful sight. The first thing they did was get those godawful clothes off us and then wash us in hot water. Nothing ever felt so good.

"They had to cut my boots off. I couldn't feel anything in my feet. When they got the boots off, I looked down at my socks and they were soaked in blood. I was afraid they were going to amputate my feet. They rubbed them with some sort of cream and then bandaged them.

"I asked the medic if they were going to have to cut off my feet. He said, 'Lieutenant, your feet are frozen. But I think we can save then.' I thought about that line that went, 'I thought I had trouble because I had no shoes until I saw a man who had no feet.'

"They wouldn't give us anything to eat at first but some kind of hot broth. 'Course after living on rice and water, it tasted pretty good. All I could think about was a big plate of fried chicken and hot biscuits. I'd lost about thirty pounds.

"Before they shipped me back to Japan, a chaplain came by one day. He said, 'God must have something left for you to do. It's a miracle you got through this.'

"He took my hand and said, 'You were spared, son, when so many others haven't been. Know that God has a plan for you. Follow where He leads you.'

"I was sort of embarrassed to think what I thought after he said that, but I couldn't help myself. I thought, 'If he'll just lead me back to Georgia and a fried chicken dinner, I'll be the happiest man alive. . . .' "

CHAPTER
6

I LIVED WITH MY FATHER ONLY SIX YEARS, THE FIRST SIX years of my life, but I remember vividly so many of his characteristics, and I still find myself emulating many of them. The tie between many fathers and their sons is that enduring, I suppose. My mother taught me my *ABC*s. From my father, I learned the glories of going to the bathroom outside.

Perhaps this is just a Southern thing, but I have known many men who prefer relieving themselves out of doors rather than performing this bodily function in the impersonal setting of a modern-day toilet.

I can't explain this, but I, too, share the desire to go to the bathroom outdoors whenever it is convenient, and convenience usually depends on such things as weather conditions and the amount of privacy available.

I have a friend, a fellow Georgian, who learned outdoor pottying from his father.

"When I was in the first grade," he told me once, "the teacher asked me what I wanted to do when I grew up. I said that when I grew up I wanted to drink beer and pee outside like my daddy.

"The teacher sent a note home with me, asking for a counseling session with my father. When she told him what I said and chastised him a bit for putting such things in my head, Daddy said, 'My daddy peed outside, and his daddy before him. If my boy follows in my footsteps, he will be merely carrying on a great family tradition.'"

When Daddy came home from Korea, he could choose any post he wanted. Such comes from being an ex-prisoner of war. He chose Fort Benning, where he would become athletic officer and coach of the post baseball and basketball teams. We bought a new house in Columbus, Georgia, and there were woods in the back.

Before retiring each night, Daddy usually would announce he was going out for a breath of air. What he really did out there was go to the bathroom on one of the pine trees. If I happened to be up at the time—and usually I was, having become a night person early in life—I would accompany him.

"Will this hurt the tree, Daddy?" I asked.

"People peed on trees for thousands of years before we had toilets," he explained.

"Did cowboys pee on trees?" I wondered.

"Mostly on cactus," Daddy went on.

I developed quite a hero worship for Roy Rogers, King of the Cowboys, when I was five or six. One day, I was being Roy out in the backyard and it became necessary to go to the bathroom. Outlaws and Indians have to wait when a five-year-old Roy Rogers is called by nature.

I dismounted my broomstick, Trigger, and picked out an unassuming tree. As I was relieving myself, my mother came walking out to hang clothes on the line.

She spotted me and, with a horrified look on her face, asked, "What do you think you are doing, young man?" When my mother was happy, she called me by my name, or something like "sugar" or "sweetie." She always used "young man" in reference to me when she was angry.

"I'm peeing on a tree," I replied. I didn't see any good reason for denial, since she was only a few feet away from me and there I stood with my privates in my hand.

"And why are you doing that?" she demanded.

"Because we don't have any cactuses," I said, returning things to their proper place, zipping my pants back up, and riding away on Trigger to continue my involvement with the outlaws and Indians.

Mother didn't say anything else. She must have thought there was some logic to my explanation, but was too busy trying to figure out what on earth it could be to continue to berate my actions.

My grandfather also peed outside on occasion, and so did my uncles and male cousins. My childhood friends did the same thing. After Boy Scout meetings in Moreland, it was fun to go up in front of the Methodist Church and pee on the road that ran downhill. The idea was to see whose stream would stay on the road the longest.

Once I held out all day so that I would have a better chance in the peeing contest after a Boy Scout meeting. We all went to the front of the church, where it was very dark and absolute privacy was maintainable. We could all run behind the church and hide if anybody happened to come by.

It was no contest that evening. If my stream hadn't eventually run into the Atlanta and West Point railroad station at the bottom of the hill, it might have even passed the scout hut and almost made it up the hill to David Covin's house. I think that going to the bathroom outside gives a man a certain closeness to nature.

Some people spend a lot of money on camping equipment and spend weeks in the wilderness when they could save themselves a lot of trouble simply by occasionally going out in their backyards to pee. They would get the same benefits as they get from camping and wouldn't have to sleep on the ground or suffer from insect bites and pinestraw and grit in their eggs every morning.

Fathers are also important to sons in learning the ropes around public restrooms. I have noticed that over the past several years they have begun to put lower urinals in public restrooms for children and short people.

This was not always the case, however. Often, I went into public restrooms with my daddy at such events as ball games and movies, and I could not reach the urinal, so he would pick me up and hold me high enough to finish my business. It was a big day in my life when Daddy took me into a restroom at a movie and I was able to hit the target without him holding me up. I simply took a step back and arched it over the side of the urinal. Daddy was very proud of me, and I was very proud of myself, so much so that when we sat back down in the movie with my mother, I said in a loud voice, "Mother! I can pee by myself!" That got a bigger laugh from the audience than Judy Canova was getting on the screen.

I learned to wear boxer shorts from my father. He wore army-issue boxer shorts. Under no circumstances did he wear jockey shorts, which is what my mother tried to get me to wear.

"I want shorts like Daddy's," I would complain when she tried to put me in jockey shorts. I wasn't even impressed when she bought me some Roy Rogers jockey shorts with pictures of Roy, Dale, Trigger, and Bullet on them. I couldn't speak for the rest of the family, but I was certain Roy Rogers didn't wear jockey shorts, and I figure his picture on a pair of jockey shorts was just some clever adult ruse to trick a child into wearing unsuitable underwear.

I have carried my aversion to jockey shorts into adulthood. Jim Palmer might be sexy to women in those skimpy little undershorts he models, but I remain loyal to those comfortable—albeit baggy— undershorts that provide more room than jockey shorts and will never ride up when it gets hot. I doubt any studies have been done on such a thing, but I would wager that a great many crimes of passion have been committed because some guy's jockey shorts have ridden up on a hot day and caused him great discomfort and his fuse to be greatly shortened.

I remember how my daddy smelled after he shaved each morning. He smelled like Old Spice. I don't care what Pete Rose and Aqua-Velva say, when a man wants to smell like a man, he wears Old Spice. I still keep a bottle of Old Spice in my bathroom. I admit I am mostly a Gray Flannel man, having been introduced to that fragrance by my third wife, whose daddy wore Gray Flannel, but I still pull out my Old Spice occasionally and rub a couple of splashes onto my face. It reminds me of Daddy.

His favorite food was fried salmon patties with hot biscuits and gravy. Mother cooked it at least once a week.

"Mahvelous salmon [he pronounced it as God intended and as the spelling insists, "sal-mon," not "sa-mon"] patties," he would roar across the table.

Occasionally I have convinced wives to prepare the same meal for me. And I will go to my grave insisting the correct pronunciation is "sal-mon."

Daddy drank more ice water than any man alive. We were driving once through a hot Georgia summer afternoon. He stopped for gas and asked the man if he had any ice water available. This is pre-OPEC, of course, when gasoline was eighteen cents a gallon and service stations still cleaned your windshield, checked your oil, and were friendly about it and occasionally even gave you plates and dishes for gasoline purchases.

The man at the service station came out with a

cup of water. Daddy gulped it down and asked, please, for another. When it came time to pay his bill, the man said, "That's five dollars for the gas and a dime for the water." Daddy was stunned.

"You have charged me a dime for two sips of water?" he asked.

The man assured him that he had.

"In the name of God," Daddy said, "that's the same thing you get for a 'dope' [which is what he called any soft drink]."

"If you feel that way about it," the man said, "keep your damn dime."

"No," said Daddy, "if you're so hard up you've got to sell water, then I want you to have it. But I shall suggest in my prayers, it would be altogether fitting if your well ran dry. Good day."

The primary reason I have been able to avoid drinking Perrier is because I am certain my father would have considered paying $1.50 for a bottle of water outrageous.

Daddy's favorite actress was Joan Crawford. I was appalled at *Mommie Dearest* and I thought Faye Dunaway was atrocious in the title role of the movie.

Daddy, when he wasn't in uniform, wore bow ties. Bow ties are coming back, and, recently, I bought myself one. When I figure out how to tie it, I will wear it.

Daddy hated beets. So do I. Daddy loved George Patton. I have seen the Patton movie at least a dozen times and have read two biographies.

Daddy snored. I used to practice snoring after I

went to bed so I could be like Daddy. Now, I don't have to practice. He would be proud of my snoring.

Daddy was a Dodger fan. I still am.

Daddy went to the University of Georgia. So did I.

Daddy was a Methodist. So am I.

Daddy got fat after he got back from Korea. The Lord had led him to numerous heaping plates of fried chicken. I was a skinny kid all the way through high school and college. Afterwards, I began to put on weight. The more I gained, the more I looked like my daddy. It was only after he died that I did something about my weight. But he used to call himself "Chief Two-Belly," and that hint of a second paunch below my stomach is still there and will remain.

I got Daddy's skinny legs and big feet. I got his eyes, green, and his fair, freckled skin. I got his hair. Daddy would have never grown bald. My barber has assured me I won't either.

My daddy taught me to laugh. He sang me funny songs when I was a child.

My favorites were those with military themes, such as:

> *There's a soldier in the grass,*
> *With a bullet in his ass,*
> *Get it out, get it out*
> *Like a good Girl Scout.*

Then there was a marching cadence:

> *See that soldier,*
> *Big and mean,*

> *See that soldier,*
> *Big and mean,*
> *Somebody peed in his canteen,*
> *Somebody peed in his canteen.*
> *Go to your left, your right,*
> *your left,*
> *Go to your left, your right,*
> *your left.*

Unfortunately, one thing I didn't inherit from my father was his musical ability. I had a difficult time playing sticks in the third-grade rhythm band, and I can't sing a lick. But I can talk like Daddy did. As a matter of fact, I can talk exactly like he did. It is impossible to re-create that voice in print, but my impression of Daddy is impeccable. He had pet phrases. "Mahvelous," of course. When he was astounded by something, Daddy would say, "In the name of God!"

Instead of "every" he said "evey," as "Eveything is going to be all right."

He preferred the British pronunciation of certain words. He didn't say "cem-i-terry," he said "cem-i-tree." He didn't say "mil-i-terry." He said, "mil-i-tree." I had a stepbrother named Bob. When Daddy would speak to him, he would say, "Roh-but, Roh-but, Roh-but."

He referred to me as "Lewis Junior," and he would string out the junior into "June-yuh." "Won-duh-ful" sometimes was substituted for "mahvelous."

"Great God!" was a substitute, I just remembered, for his astounded "In the name of God!"

He spoke loudly. He was one of those people who couldn't whisper even if he tried.

His voice commanded attention. He was never ignored in his life. When he spoke from a dais or a pulpit, his voice filled the room, the words catapulted from his mouth and caromed off the walls.

"Nobody can defeat the American soldier!" he would roar to his listeners. "The American army is the finest military machine the world has ever seen! And George Patton was right. We are going to have to fight the Rooshans [his word for Russians] sooner or later, and I don't know why we didn't do it while we were still over there!"

Later, after Daddy had died, I received a letter from one of his former students at a north Georgia mountain high school. Over the years I have been amazed to find out all the places he taught and worked. He could, in fact, talk his way into and out of almost any situation. The former student wrote, "One thing I always will remember about your daddy is he had morning devotion each day, and his prayers were just great! They were even funny, and he would always end them with, '. . . And, Lord, please keep us safe from the Rooshans.' "

He had a number of Rooshan stories from the war. "When we got to Berlin in forty-five," he would begin, "I pulled detention duty. I had two or three hundred Rooshans in the compound for doing one thing or another.

"I never saw people like the Rooshans. They were the craziest bunch of people I ever ran into in my life. We had a high fence around the compound with barbed wire on top. They would stay in there until they saw somebody ride by on a bicycle outside. They were fascinated by bicycles. They'd just climb that fence like it wasn't there, chase down whoever was on the bicycle and knock him off. Then, they'd ride around on the bicycle for a little while and then put it down and climb back over the fence into the compound.

"And I'll tell you something, the Rooshan women were just as tough as the Rooshan men and just as ugly, too. The biggest problem we had with 'em was to convince them not to drink out of the toilets. They thought they were water fountains. And one day, we're going to have to fight 'em. Lord, I'd hate to have to fight some of those Rooshan women."

He drank buttermilk with every meal, and he was fond of his "Snellville midnight milkshake." I couldn't drink buttermilk as a child, and I still can't drink it. Not only is the taste horribly sour, but there is nothing that looks worse than a glass after it has had buttermilk in it.

"In the name of God, son," he would say to me when I turned up my nose at buttermilk, "there is nothing better in this world than a cold glass of buttermilk. I am convinced it will heal the sick and raise the dead."

Some of those memories are nearly forty years old, but they are indelible and they are a comfort.

To love someone unconditionally—as I loved Daddy—is to remember each detail of their personage, to remember isolated and long-past moments together, to remember nuances that made such an object of love unique and impossible to replace.

That is why I remember, and cherish, the memories of the man's hair, his smell, his likes and dislikes, his speech, and his idiosyncracies.

We had such a little time together. War took him away.

Then he came back for a short time before he was gone again. He never would return on a full-time basis.

Maybe that is why each of the nuances, each of the jokes and stories, each of the memories is so priceless to me. I have some pictures of my father. I have that packet of war records. I have the flag that was across his casket. I have his Bronze Star and his Purple Hearts in a frame and they hang on my wall.

But what I don't have anymore is him. There will be no new memories made. That is why I cling to those I have with such tenacity.

After Korea, after the ecstasy of the homecoming, there were only a few months left of what was once my family.

CHAPTER
7

FROM THE *GRANTVILLE GAZETTE*, FRIDAY, MAY *11, 1951:*

A Georgia officer, Capt. Lewis Grizzard, recently returned home from the Korean battlefront, will be the guest speaker at the third meeting of the Grantville Men's Club next Monday night. The meeting will be held at the high school and following the luncheon, Capt. Grizzard will tell of some of his experiences at the front in the Far East.

Capt. Grizzard, a former schoolteacher and veteran of fighting in Europe as well as in the Far East, had the unusual experience of being wounded and then nursed by the same enemy.

Capt. Grizzard and a fellow soldier lived for sixteen days in a hole in the hills of North Korea with a Chinese member of the North Korean army who tended to their wounds and foraged for their food.

Henry Jackson, president of the Men's Club, is urging every

*man in town to attend this meeting as the guest speaker has a
great fund of experiences and stories to relate.*

Robert Dews knew my daddy at Fort Benning.
He, too, was a World War II and Korean War veteran. Sergeant Dews now lives in Edison and is a
writer. We have corresponded often. He always re-
fers to Daddy as "the Captain." He is one of the
few I have been able to contact in research for this
book who was with Daddy when the end of his
army career came.

Want a rather poignant omen? To better understand Korea and what it meant to the men who
fought there, before sitting down to write, I read a
book entitled *The Korean War: Pusan to Chosin,* an oral
history by Donald Knox. Knox is to Korea what
Studs Terkel is to World War II in his oral history of
that war, *"The Good War".*

Knox's work involves interviews with hundreds
of men who fought in Korea. I bought the book and
opened it, at random, in the middle. The first interview I saw was that of Sergeant Robert Dews.

Sergeant Dews returned from Korea to Fort Benning in August 1951. Daddy had sufficiently recovered from his experience to have been named athletic officer at the post. Dews was a ball player. He
was also a sick man. The Korean experience had
made a boozer out of him, too.

"I was in and out of the hospital at least a year
after I got back," he recalls. "They let me out on
weekends, and like the other Korea boys, I drank all
weekend, and then reported back on Monday, hung

over and sick. They would get me well again to be ready for another weekend of drinking."

Sergeant Dews remembers me from Fort Benning. "You were always at the Captain's side at ball games."

He remembers my mother.

"Christine was so pretty. That black hair."

He even remembers the car we had.

"It was an old Hudson. The Captain called it The Blue Goose."

And his memories of my daddy are priceless to me.

"The Captain outranked me, but we were kindred souls. He was my friend. I don't know if you remember much about your daddy back then," he once said to me, "but he was some kind of man. He stood about six-two, and there was just something about his presence in a room. He took it over the minute he walked in."

I wanted to know about the "kindred souls" things.

"The Captain had it rough in Korea. You know all about that," Sergeant Dews went on. "There just wasn't much of a rehabilitation program. Things were different back then. A soldier was supposed to be able to handle anything that came his way.

"Well, I'm sure you know the Captain was drinking a lot, just like the rest of us. But the Captain was so emotional. He had nightmares, and that on top of all his service in World War II. God only knows how many good men he saw get it.

"You mix a lot of emotion with booze and you've got trouble, especially if you are walking a tightrope to begin with. I tried to take care of the Captain, and he tried to take care of me. When I was in no shape to drive—after I got out of the hospital and I'd been nursing on a bottle all day—he'd put me in the Blue Goose and get me the hell off the post. When the walls were closing in on him, I'd put him in my red Jeep. We stuck together."

But I had heard so many stories about how popular he was after Korea. There were the countless speech and interview requests my mother had told me about.

"I think that was one of the Captain's problems," said Sergeant Dews. "He was getting all sorts of offers to speak, to civic clubs, ladies' clubs, you name it. He was a returning war hero.

"I think some of the other officers at Benning were jealous of him. He was getting all the attention. They started watching his every move, and they came down hard on him every chance they got.

"I'll tell you another problem he had. He was very popular with the enlisted men, and the other officers didn't like that. You know how he was. He always had a joke to tell. He got people to react because they liked him, not because he was their superior officer.

"He helped a lot of those kids back from the war when the army wouldn't do a thing for them. He even moved a couple of the boys in with him at your house in Columbus, and put up their wives, too, and tried to help the wives understand what their husbands were going through."

Soon, Daddy lost Sergeant Dews at Benning.

Dews was a star baseball player, and the commander at Fort McPherson in Atlanta had him transferred there to play on the Fort Mac team.

"I hated to leave the Captain, and he hated me to leave, but orders were orders. He needed somebody he could confide in, tell his troubles to. Once, he even drove up to Fort Mac during a ball game and sat right down on the bench with me and told me the nightmares were getting worse, the drinking even harder to control. You know who was sitting next to me? A general, that's who. But the Captain didn't care. He needed to talk."

Several months ago, I managed to get what remained of Daddy's military records from the National Military Records Center in St. Louis. I was informed some of his records had been lost in a fire. His Certificate of Military Service indicates his second term of service—after receiving an honorable discharge from the first in order to accept his battlefield commission—commenced 19 April 1945. It ended 1 April 1953. "Service was terminated," the certificate said, "by other than honorable means."

"All we ever heard up at Fort Mac," said Sergeant Dews, "was that he had been court-martialed and had left the army. I went into headquarters one day and asked about him, and I was told to stay out of it, that the Captain was in the middle of proceedings.

"But then later, I found out there had been no court-martial. I think what happened is they held the threat of a court-martial over him, and he was just in no shape to fight for his military life. Once the army gets the bit in its mouth or a wild hair up its ass about something they don't like, they can come down very hard."

We had a little house in Columbus. I had a dog. The dog's name was Snowfall. Life was making sense to me again. My daddy and my mother were in the same house again, and we went places together, and whatever Korea was, I decided it was over.

My memories from that time, the early months in Columbus and Fort Benning after Daddy returned from Korea, are the only real memories I have of the family together. They come in flashes.

We used to eat at Pritchett's Catfish House in Columbus. "All the fried catfish you can eat, $2.95." I always sat in the booth next to Daddy while he pulled the bones out of my catfish. I drank 7-Ups.

Snowball got sick. Daddy took him to the vet. I kept asking about my dog. Daddy said he would be back soon. We were at Pritchett's eating catfish a week or so later.

I asked about Snowball again.

Mother looked at Daddy.

"You've got to tell him," she said.

He pulled me over into his lap and put his hand behind my head and began stroking my hair.

"Snowball had pneumonia," he said. "The dog doctor said he couldn't make him well again, and Snowball died."

"Do dogs go to heaven, Daddy?" I asked.

"I'm sure they do," he answered.

Later that night I was crying about my dog in

bed. Daddy came in, put his arms around me and took me to his bed and held me closely to him.

"I'll get you another dog," he said. He never did, because there wasn't that much time left, but I think he otherwise would have. I really do.

I began to notice a few changes. I mentioned my parents had separate bedrooms, but at the time that didn't seem unnatural to me. Plus, I had a choice when there was thunder and lightning as to whose bed I would retreat.

But there began loud conversations. And Daddy began to cry a lot. He would make telephone calls and he would cry into the phone.

Some nights, when I was sleeping with him, I would rub the back of his head. I could feel things in the back of his head. I asked him what they were.

"Shrapnel," he said.

He tried to explain about things exploding and men getting killed. And he would begin crying again and I would cry with him.

People came to our house. I didn't know who they were. If Daddy wasn't there, they would argue with Mother.

One night a man knocked on our door. Daddy wasn't home. The man demanded to see him. Mother said he wasn't there. He didn't believe her. They argued.

He said something about Daddy owing him some money. He said if Daddy didn't pay him back, he was going to kill him. My Uncle Frank, the lawyer, came to visit us. He and Daddy talked for hours.

They wouldn't let me stay in the room with them while they were talking.

My Uncle Wesley came, and he and Daddy talked for a long time, too.

My Aunt Una, who loved my daddy, told me, "For some reason—and we never found out why—he began to borrow a lot of money from people. He even borrowed from enlisted men, and an officer just doesn't do that sort of thing.

"People started coming to your house and demanding to see him because he owed them money. They were making life miserable for your mother and she couldn't seem to do anything to help him, or to find out what his problem was.

"We didn't know if he was being blackmailed or what, but your Uncle Frank once traced some of his borrowings and said your daddy went through $50,000 in six months. We didn't know what to think and he wouldn't talk to anybody about why he was doing all that.

"He finally had to leave Benning because there were so many people after him to pay back the money. I guess he just had to go AWOL, and that's when the army kicked him out."

My Aunt Rufy, Daddy's sister and the last surviving member of his family, said, "There hasn't been a day passed in the last thirty years, I didn't wonder what happened to Lewis. But he never would tell me anything, either."

I have heard things over the years. I heard he had gotten into some trouble over a real estate deal when we were in Camp Chaffee, Arkansas. There is nobody left to confirm or deny that.

One of my late uncles once told me Daddy had been involved in taking some of the payroll at Fort Benning. There apparently are no records of that, either.

Sergeant Dews said it was his nerves. He used the word "tightrope."

Before he died, I asked Daddy a thousand times, "What is wrong? Why can't you stay sober? Why can't you stay in one place? What can be so bad you can't talk about it?"

He never would answer me directly, but there was that once. I was fifteen or sixteen. He had remarried a kind woman named Betty, who loved him, too. They had a house in East Point, a suburb of Atlanta.

I would go and visit on weekends. Betty was nice to me, and I hoped Daddy would stay with her. Then I would have him close by and there would be some constancy in his life and in our relationship.

But he couldn't cut it. He went out on another of his benders. Betty couldn't take it anymore, and he was left to his own wits again.

Sometime after that, I visited him for a weekend in Atlanta. For the first time in my life I talked to him hard. I think he was shocked. He had not lived with me since I was six. I think he was shocked he couldn't flower things over for me anymore. I had so wanted him to stay with Betty so I would always know where he was.

So I put my hands in his, and I begged him to tell me what was wrong. I told him I didn't care what it was, that I loved him, and I wanted him to be okay. That's the very word I used—okay.

He began crying. He began sobbing. I really think he wanted to tell me. I think he always had wanted to tell somebody, but he never had the courage.

"I made a mistake once," he said. "A bad mistake."

"What did you do? Daddy, please tell me."

There was a silence.

"I made a terrible mistake," he said.

That's all I ever got. The man died, so far as I know, with his secret.

My mother is old now and very sick. My one attempt to interrogate her for this book failed miserably.

"Mother," I said to her, "was there something that happened to Daddy that caused him to leave that I didn't know about?"

There was some pain in her voice as she answered. What happened to her and my father happened thirty-five years ago, but I could still hear some of the pain.

"It was just all that drinking he did, son," Mother said. "But you ought not to go digging all that out again."

My aunts had said that to me, too. I hope they understand why I had to.

So what had he meant? What terrible, black secret did he have? The certificate said, "Other than honorable." Daddy never got a single benefit from the army, despite service that was heroic. What could he have done to deserve being ridden out with nothing to show for that heroism?

I have come to the point of this book, I wish I had something concrete to reveal. But I don't.

I will only say that as I have mentioned before, I have proof in black and white that my daddy was a great man, a great soldier, and, if you will allow me, a great American. I don't care what he did. He was owed more than he got, which was nothing.

Maybe he did want to tell me something that night years ago when I held his hands and begged him.

And maybe he did tell me something.

But what could it have been? Had he somehow failed in battle? Did he do something so dreadfully wrong that morning in Unsan that he cost other men their lives?

Want more speculation? He collaborated with the enemy. Farfetched, sure, but when there are no answers whatsoever, one can't help but think the unthinkable.

Did he kill somebody? Did he rob or cheat somebody? In these later times, the unthinkable of days past becomes certainly not commonplace, but more visible to the public eye.

Was he a child molester? Or guilty of cowardice? Was he a homosexual?

I can think of no more unthinkables. No matter. Whatever his sin, his secret, I loved him—and I love him—anyway.

I think that is what is referred to today as unconditional love.

CHAPTER
8

MY FIRST-GRADE TEACHER AT ROSEMONT ELEMENTARY School in Columbus was Mrs. Huff. She was an older lady, a widow, and I remember her as being kind and especially patient in art class with students like me who, beyond molding mud cakes after a rain, had no artistic ability whatsoever. We were asked one day to draw a picture of the houses we lived in. Mrs. Huff looked at mine and said, "Oh, you live in a teepee?"

I had attempted to draw a simple 3 BR Rnch, as the classifieds say, but in trying to slope the roof, I had made it a bit too pointed.

I had the same trouble with clay modeling. Mrs. Huff asked us to make a dog out of modeling clay. "I think you have a few parts missing from your dog," said Mrs. Huff when she saw my completed work.

"What parts?" I asked.

"For starters," Mrs. Huff answered, "feet, legs, tail, and a head."

I still remember some of my classmates. There was a kid named Joseph Something-or-other, whose head was too big for the rest of his body. Think of Mr. Potato Head's physique and that was Joseph.

Joseph's nose was always running. It didn't matter how many times Mrs. Huff told Joseph to blow his nose, it would start running again. It was another kid, Skeeter, who taught me one of my earlier bad words, which was *snot*. Snot isn't all that bad compared to what people say today on television, but Skeeter was always calling Joseph "Snotnose." One day I came home from school and my mother asked me what I had learned that day.

"A new word," I answered.

"Oh," she replied, "and what word is that?"

"*Snot,*" I said.

"Where did you learn an awful word like that?" Mother demanded. "I know Mrs. Huff didn't teach it to you."

"Skeeter taught it to me," I said. "It's that stuff that's always coming out of Joseph's nose."

Mother told Daddy when he came home that I had learned the word *snot.* That evening he taught me some more new words, like *booger* and *poot.*

My daddy spoiled me, I admit, those last years in Columbus. Not only did he teach me new words, but if I didn't like what Mother had prepared for dinner, he would take me out for a hamburger and a milkshake.

I sat on the bench, or in his lap, when he coached a ball game while his players would load me with Cokes and candy. Daddy bought me a baseball uniform. I got to take a few cuts of my own when his team took batting practice.

We went to movies. There was no X or R or PG in those days. There was just Joel McCrea and Randolph Scott and Roy and Gene. I was never that much of a Gene Autry fan, however. He sang too much and never really settled down with one woman like Roy did with Dale.

We lived in a pleasant little subdivision in Columbus. What I remember most about our house was we had a screen door, the outline of a flamingo molded inside it. I thought it gave our house a certain panache, since none of the other people on the street had a flamingo in their screen doors.

We lived at the top of a big hill. The neighbors' kids and I took turns riding our wagons to the bottom of the hill and then pulling them back to the top. Before he died, Snowball would copilot in my wagon with me. After Snowball died, a cat followed me home one day and I took it for a ride in my wagon. The cat became frightened and leaped on my head as I was attempting to maneuver my wagon down the treacherous, hilly course.

My vision was completely blocked and I ran my wagon into a mailbox. In the collision, I fell out of the wagon and skinned my knee. It bled profusely and my mother covered it with iodine, which made it hurt and burn just that much more. I dislike cats to this day.

* * *

There was a Peeping Tom in the neighborhood. I heard the parents of some of my friends talking about him. One Sunday afternoon I was outside playing and I noticed a number of adult men had gathered in front of a neighbor's house. I investigated.

The men had surrounded a frightened black man who was lying on the ground. He, they said, was the Peeping Tom. Somebody had called the police. The men were making certain Peeping Tom wouldn't run away.

One of the men kicked him and called him a "nigger." Some of the other men spat on him.

When my daddy came home I told him somebody had caught a "nigger" in the neighborhood and had been kicking and spitting on him.

" 'Nigger' is a bad word," he said. I never knew the man ever to utter a racist remark.

I was delighted to have learned another one.

"I don't want to hear you use it anymore," Daddy went on. I asked him why. "Because you can hurt somebody's feelings by using that word. Don't use it around Louise," he explained.

Louise was a giant black woman who came by a couple of days a week to help out in the house. I loved Louise. She used to pick me up with those giant arms of hers and take on over me. She always baked a couple of cakes each week and she let me take to the leftover batter in the bowl with a spoon.

"Is Louise a nigger, Daddy?" I asked.

"Louise is 'colored.' You should say 'colored.' Never say 'nigger.' "

Louise died a few weeks after that incident. Daddy took mother and me to the funeral; we were the only white people there. Daddy sang "It Is No Secret (What God Can Do)" and after the funeral, they laid out a huge spread of fried chicken and other delights outside the church.

"Louise sho' did think a lot of yo' little boy, Captain Grizzard," one of the mourners said to Daddy.

"She was like one of the family to us," Daddy said.

"I never said 'nigger' around Louise," I told everyone proudly. I could see the horror in Daddy's face.

The lady smiled and rubbed her hand across my head. "Y'all is fine white folks," she said.

They gave Daddy a sack of chicken to take home with him as we left. "Do colored people go to the same heaven as us?" I asked Daddy.

"I'm sure they do, son," he answered.

I was happy to know that. Now there was somebody to look after Snowball.

It was spring and Mother began allowing me to walk to school with my friends. I took it as a great leap toward maturity. Kids whose mothers brought them to school were looked down upon as—I am certain I remember the term correctly—"fraidy cats." To be called a fraidy cat was horrible. Joseph's mother was still driving him to school and Skeeter called him a "snot-nosed fraidy cat." Skeeter was quite a verbal child to be only six. I wonder if he wound up in advertising.

The day was passing as it usually passed. I sat in

the front of one of the rows. Mrs. Huff was teaching an afternoon lesson. There was a knock on the door. Mrs. Huff went over and opened it. There stood Daddy.

They were friends, Mrs. Huff and Daddy. We often picked her up on Sundays for lunch—me, my teacher, my daddy, and my mother. Mrs. Huff was as taken by Daddy's charm as everybody else. He even confided in her that he was having problems. What I remember is she gave him a book to read. The book was *The Power of Positive Thinking* by Norman Vincent Peale. Years later, I found the book in a box my mother had tossed back in a closet in our home in Moreland. The book had an inscription. It read: "May God guide you always—Sarah Huff."

Daddy whispered something to my teacher. She motioned for me to come to my desk.

"Go with your daddy," she said. "I'll see you tomorrow."

I gathered my books, walked outside with Daddy, and got into the blue Hudson. I would never return to Mrs. Huff or Rosemont School.

"Where are we going?" I asked Daddy.

"To your Aunt Rufy's in Atlanta," he answered.

"Is Mother coming with us?"

"No," he said.

Mother was substitute teaching at another school that week. Daddy had picked me up the previous couple of days after school, and we had driven over to bring Mother home. I remember wondering how she would get home if we weren't there to give her a ride.

I was uneasy leaving without her. Daddy didn't

seem himself, for one thing. The more I questioned him about Mother, the shorter he became with me. I had never known a single instance where Daddy seemed displeased with me.

"Don't ask me any more questions," he said. He almost snapped.

We drove to Rufy's house in Atlanta. They put me to bed after dinner. I couldn't go to sleep. I heard Daddy and Rufy arguing in the next room.

I didn't realize the gravity of the situation at the moment, of course, but what was happening was my daddy was going AWOL from the army. He was running away from whatever it was that was chasing him into oblivion. And he was taking me with him. He was, for all practical purposes, kidnapping me.

I wondered later why he was obviously prepared to leave everything else behind him, including his wife and his career, but he obviously wasn't prepared to leave me. He had to know what taking me away would do to my mother. He had to know that if he were trying to hide—from debtors or whatever —having a six-year-old boy tagging along would make it much harder for him to stay hidden.

So why would he want me with him? Why, in this moment of utter desperation, would he want me in the midst of it?

Again, I can only speculate. So many of the questions I ask myself now did not seem to be of import when he was still alive to answer them.

Maybe he took me to cushion the blow somehow. Perhaps he knew how hard it would be to leave my mother, to leave his career. Maybe he thought that if I were with him, he at least would have some link to that which he had left behind.

Maybe. Perhaps. Desperation rarely knows any concrete explanations.

Aunt Rufy drove us to the train station in Atlanta. We left the Hudson behind. Rufy said to Daddy, "You had better call Christine. She'll be worried to death."

"I will," he promised her.

We rode the train all night. When we got off I asked Daddy where we were.

"Portsmouth, Virginia," he answered me.

We stayed with some of Daddy's relatives I'd never seen before. They were his cousins. They had a son a couple of years older than I. He went to school every morning, but I didn't. The kid couldn't understand why he had to go and I didn't, and, frankly, neither did I.

I was confused. I was frightened. I missed my mother. I missed my friends at school. I had been yanked out of my security again.

And what my mother obviously was going through—the agony and the terror she must have felt when she discovered the both of us gone.

She called Rufy first. Rufy said Daddy had told her he had to get away, that the world was caving in around him. Rufy said he told her he was taking me to Savannah and would call her as soon as he got there. Rufy said he had promised to call.

But there had been no call. Mother was out of her mind. She called Uncle Frank, the lawyer. He persuaded her not to call the police. He said he would find me and Daddy.

We were in Portsmouth a week. A hurricane came through. Small craft were washed in front of the house in which we were staying. Trees were uprooted. When the hurricane hit with its full force, Daddy and I were in an upstairs bedroom together. I remember the windows rattling, the beams of the house groaning against the power of the wind.

I was frightened. I cried. I begged for my mother. Daddy held me. He didn't speak. He just held me.

Uncle Frank called all the relatives. He finally located us in Portsmouth. The relatives told Frank Daddy had not explained that he was AWOL or that my mother had no idea of our whereabouts.

Uncle Frank drove Mother to Portsmouth. They drove all night.

I was overjoyed to see her. I thought her presence meant things would go back to normal. I thought I would be back in Mrs. Huff's class the next day.

I was wrong. Mother screamed. She cried. She lashed out at Daddy. I had never witnessed such things before. Frank tried to calm her. He couldn't. I tugged at the bottom of her dress from on my knees and begged her not to scream anymore.

Daddy was a beaten man. He had no explanation for what he had done. I could still picture him sitting in a kitchen chair, his hands folded on his knees, his stare directed at the floor.

"Don't hate me, Christine" is all he could say.

"I *do* hate you!" Mother tore on.

The ravings continued into the night. Uncle Frank finally was able to bring Mother to at least a temporary halt. Frank talked to Daddy about the army.

"Let them know where you are," he said. "With your record, they shouldn't press charges if you go back to the post as quickly as you can."

Daddy agreed to do what Uncle Frank said. He never did, so far as I know, however. All that is clear is that at some point, the army cut Daddy loose and took his benefits away. There were no charges, again, at least so far as I know. Maybe that is the deal the army gave the man who came out of that hole in Korea.

The next morning, I got into Uncle Frank's car with my mother. Daddy squeezed me—it was a comparable squeeze to that he offered the day he left for Korea—and said, as he always said, "Be a good soldier."

That was it. There was no more family. No more "Tennessee Waltz." Daddy never went back to the army and Mother never went back to Daddy.

I didn't understand the separation, of course. All Mother would tell me was that Daddy was "a sick man." If he were sick, I thought to myself, why wasn't he in bed? Mother always made me go to bed when I was sick.

An emptiness hit me. It hit me in the pit of my stomach. My life suddenly had lost all its sense of security. Mother cried a lot. I asked for things. Mother said we didn't have enough money. I slept beside her every night. I wouldn't even go into Daddy's room anymore. It made me miss him that much more.

Mother sold our house. She packed our belong-

ings and we took the *Man O' War* from Columbus to
Atlanta. Aunt Rufy picked us up at the station.

"What are you going to do, Christine?" she asked
my mother.

Mother said she didn't know. She said she had to
find a way to take care of me.

"Do you think Lewis will ever straighten out?"
Aunt Rufy asked. (That phrase "straighten out" al-
ways seemed to come up when adults talked about
Daddy.)

"I don't know, Rufy," my mother said. "I don't
know."

I listened from the backseat of the car. The fear
strengthened inside me. Even at six, I realized the
gravity of the situation. Mother screamed at Daddy.
Daddy cried. Then Daddy took me away, and then
Mother came and got me and, all of a sudden,
Daddy wasn't around anymore. No sense of ill-be-
ing has ever been as strong in me as the one that
gripped me when it became evident the separation
of my mother and Daddy was to be a long-term
arrangement.

We lived with Aunt Rufy for a short time and
then Mother made up her mind. We were going
back to Moreland, where we had fled when Daddy
was in Korea. Mama Willie and Daddy Bun had the
extra bedroom.

That had to be a difficult decision for my mother,
to go back to her parents. She was forty. She had
been away from the parental nest for over twenty
years. To return would be admitting defeat, admitting her life outside the nest had been a failure.

And the change in life-style would be dramatic.

Even with all his troubles and problems, Daddy was a dynamic man with whom to share a life. She had traveled the country with him. There had been the parties, the bridge games, the nights at the officers' club. They had danced together and laughed together, and now she faced what remained of her life alone, save for me and her parents. None of us, of course, could make up for the absence of her husband and lover.

Mother said to Aunt Rufy, "I just don't know if I can go back to Moreland and live, but I don't have a choice."

"You can't give up yet," Aunt Rufy said to her. "Maybe this separation will bring Lewis to his senses."

I lived on that one line for a long time. Daddy had been gone once before and had come back, hadn't he?

Pray, I thought to myself. Pray as hard as you can and keep your eyes tightly closed and maybe one day soon, Daddy will come for us and take us away and there won't be this feeling anymore, the one that is telling me something is terribly amiss and it isn't going to get better anytime soon.

Aunt Rufy drove us the forty-five miles south from Atlanta to Moreland. Mama Willie hugged me when I got out of the car. She was a direct woman.

"He's not going to hurt you anymore, Christine," Mama Willie said to Mother. "You're home now."

And we were.

CHAPTER
9

I DID NOT DEAL VERY WELL WITH SUDDENLY HAVING NO daddy. I pouted, I cried. Mama Willie said, "Crying too much will leave dark circles under your eyes."

I didn't care. I pined for my father. "Pined" is an old word, but that was a long time ago, and it seems to fit here.

One of the main problems of being a child is you can control very little in your life. I couldn't decide the pain was so great that I simply had to see my daddy. I couldn't get into a car or on a train or a bus and go to see him. I was stuck.

My mother's family circled in protection of my mother after the separation. They turned on Daddy. They decided to protect me against him as well.

I was forbidden to talk about him in front of Mama Willie. My grandparents had a telephone by this time. When Daddy called and Mother was there, she would let me talk to him. If Mother wasn't there, and Mama Willie answered, she wouldn't.

She was a sweet and kind woman, and I think she was trying to do what she thought was best for me, but I resented it. I turned incorrigible. I went out one day in a fit of anger and broke down a number of the stalks in my grandfather's cornfield. The next morning, we were going to dig worms for a fishing trip and we had to walk through the cornfield. I had forgotten about my devastation of it the previous day.

"Look at this," he said. "Somebody broke the head off this stalk. Here's another one."

I broke into a dead run back to the house and went immediately to bed.

"Are you sick?" Mother asked.

I made a moaning noise.

In a few minutes, Mama Willie came into the room with some foul-smelling medicine. "He's constipated probably," she said to my mother.

I decided to confess my crime. That would be better than taking that god-awful medicine.

"I broke Daddy Bun's corn," said I, sobbing. "Don't tell him it was me," I begged.

She put the medicine away and wiped my tears.

"You tell him," she said.

At the supper table that night, Mama Willie announced that I had something to say.

"Mumble, mumble, mumble," I began.

"Speak up," said my grandfather.

"I broke down your cornstalks," I finally blurted out.

Daddy Bun was a quiet man whom I never once

saw lose his temper except when the Jehovah's Witnesses came around to hand out pamphlets. He said we would talk about it the next morning while we were fishing.

But he never brought it up. We caught three mud cats and four bream. Men, it always seemed to me, were much more tolerant than women.

I could tell Mother clung to some sort of hope, though likely much fainter than mine, that Daddy would, as they said, "straighten himself out."

She even risked the family's scorn by sneaking off to meet him on occasion. She had bought a 1947 Chevrolet and was able to get a full-time teaching job, first grade at Senoia, another small hamlet ten miles west of Moreland. She was paid $120 a month.

She would tell Mama Willie we were going to see Aunt Rufy in Atlanta.

Sometimes, we would meet Daddy at the Peter Pan Motel in Griffin, twenty-five miles away. A few other times, we met him in Atlanta. I loved motels. Daddy would let me jump on the beds.

They talked after they thought I was asleep. Sometimes, I faked sleep in order to listen to their every word, hoping to hear some encouragement that Daddy would come to get us soon. There was no single thing in my world that would have made me happier.

I would ask Daddy directly, "Are you going to come and get us?"

"One of these nights," he would say, "I'll be outside your window and I'll say, Christine . . . Mr. Saberaaah . . . let's go."

Those words were enchanted. I heard them over and over in my mind. Back in Moreland, I would go to sleep next to my mother hoping for those words to come out of the night.

My mother's brothers didn't like my daddy. They said he drank too much and he had hurt my mother. My Uncle Dorsey took me with him one morning to Newnan where a man was going to shoe his horse. I forget the man's name, but he said to Dorsey, "Is that a pretty good boy you've got with you there?"

Uncle Dorsey said, "Yeah, he's my sister's boy. Only thing wrong with him is he don't mind very good because he takes after his daddy."

The tears welled up inside me again. How could they talk about my daddy the way they did? Why did they want to keep me from him? My entire life centered around being with him again. And each time they said something about him, the anger and the resentment grew inside me. Daddy Bun was the only one who never stated his opinion on the matter. I found myself at his side as often as possible. He was my consolation prize for my father.

I began the second grade at Moreland School. Mother had contacted Mrs. Huff back in Columbus and she agreed to pass me despite the fact that I had been out the last six weeks of first grade.

There was something different about Moreland School and its students. The school was old and near collapse. The students were not at all like those back at Rosemont. They were rural and tough. Some came to school barefoot. They were greatly suspicious of me.

I was in Mrs. Bowers's room. She was somewhat
a legend for her sternness. She talked about Jesus a
lot. She whipped Sammy Whitten one day for talking back to her. I thought she was going to beat the
poor child to death, and I became extremely afraid
of her. Then, one day, she saved my life.

The toughest kid in school was Frankie Garfield,
who had two brothers. One day, they brought some
gunpowder to school and made a bomb and blew
out all the windows in the fourth-grade room.

Frankie caught me out on the playground one
day.

"Where you from, boy?" he asked me.

I didn't know what he meant.

"I said, 'Where you from, boy?'" he repeated
himself. "You wasn't at school here last year."

"I went to Rosemont," I said.

"Where is that?"

"Columbus," I said.

"You're one of them city boys," Frankie replied,
with a great deal of disdain in his voice.

I thought quickly. My grandfather had given me
one of his empty tobacco bags, the kind that tied up
at the top with yellow string that always hung out
of his back pocket.

"Want a sack?" I asked Frankie.

He snatched the sack away from me and then
grabbed me in a headlock. I was powerless to escape
his hold. I think Frankie would have wound up
beating me senseless—as well as keeping my sack—
had it not been for Mrs. Bowers.

She spotted him from across the playground and
came rushing over. She let Frankie have one upside

his forehead and when he let me go, she grabbed him and shook him unmercifully. I don't know if Frankie's eyes ever got back together she shook him so hard.

I was forever indebted to Mrs. Bowers after that, and I made certain that whenever I was on the playground, I stayed as close to her as possible.

It didn't take long to get around school there was something different about me. What was different was that I didn't have a daddy, or one to show to everybody else. Kids heard their parents talking, I suppose.

"Where's your daddy?" a kid asked me on the way home from school one day.

"He lives somewhere else," I answered. The tears were coming. I tried to hold them back.

"He doesn't live with you and your mother?" was the next question.

I felt terribly cornered, and I couldn't see a way out. I began to cry.

"You must be a sissy," the boy said to me. "You ain't got no daddy and you cry."

I don't think it ever hurt not to have a daddy around as much as it did at that moment. This was no adult talking to me. This was a peer, and he seemed to look down on me and consider me different because I had no father at my house.

It never stopped coming up. When word got completely around on me, I was always being grilled about the whereabouts of my father.

"He ain't dead, is he?" they would ask.

"No, he ain't dead."

"Well, where is he, then?"

"He's in the army."

"No, he ain't. My daddy said they kicked him out of the army."

"He quit."

"No, he didn't. They kicked him out."

I could never hold back the tears in such a discussion. I always cried and that always made matters worse. Daddy Bun, once again, saved me.

He was the janitor at the school. The old man had never known anything but work and that is about all he ever did. He lighted the morning fires in the stoves in the rooms, and then he went back to his twelve acres of garden in the afternoon. He was back to clean up after school. He would spread that oily, grainy substance on the wooden floors of the school and then sweep it up.

He heard one of my classmates badgering me about my daddy one afternoon.

"His daddy was a hero in the war," he told the kid. "He got shot several times, and he was even captured by the enemy, but he got away. His daddy is just sick right now, and you boys ought not to be carrying on that way. Your daddy could get sick one day, too."

That helped. And so did Mrs. Bowers, once again. She asked that everyone come back to school the next day and be prepared to stand in front of the class and tell what their fathers did for a living.

I was frightened of her assignment at first, but then she said, "And I think everybody will be interested in Lewis Grizzard's daddy because he was a hero in the war."

I beamed. My mother filled me in on as many of

the details as she could that evening, and I gave my classmates the full measure of my pride the next day at school.

"My daddy is a sheetrocker," one kid said.

"My daddy works for Cole Shop."

"My daddy works at Trimedge."

"My daddy works at the sawmill."

"My daddy," I said, "was a hero in the war."

That remains one of the brightest days of my academic career.

It got better for me. I made friends. I joined the Cub Scouts. I went to Sunday School at the Methodist Church and to Methodist Youth Fellowship (MYF) at night. I got myself a girl friend. Daddy Bun gave me a silver dollar once. I gave it to my girl friend.

Daddy still called occasionally, and as I got older Mama Willie finally relented on keeping me from him. I would also visit him occasionally, usually in Atlanta. These were visits to Wonderland. I would stand with my mother at the highway a few yards from the house and we would wave down the northbound Greyhound bus. Daddy would pick me up in Atlanta and immediately get my shoes shined and all my hair cut off. Some of the military never left him.

But they had a problem with me back at home. Whenever I went to visit Daddy, I came home Sunday nights in total agony. I missed him hard.

Sunday nights after a visit were almost too much for me to bear. I wouldn't eat. I wouldn't speak.

"He's still spoiling that child," Mama Willie would say to Mother.

But she stood by me. Whenever there was a chance for me to see Daddy, she allowed me to go. She never talked badly to me about him. She never —and it would have been easier for her, perhaps, had she been able to do such a thing—tried to turn me against him.

Daddy was working in Atlanta selling shirts at Rich's the summer between my third and fourth grades. He called and asked if I could come for maybe a month. Mother agreed.

A month! I was ecstatic. Daddy lived in an apartment building on Ponce de Leon Avenue in Atlanta, just a few blocks from Ponce de Leon Park, home of the Atlanta Crackers minor league baseball team. At games, he bought me vanilla custard ice cream, the likes of which I never have been able to find since. We even discovered where visiting teams stayed, up the street at the Georgian Terrace Hotel. Daddy took me there one afternoon before a night game and managed to get me a baseball signed by all the Little Rock Travelers.

I stayed in the apartment during the day while Daddy worked. There was a nice lady who ran the place. I watched television soap operas during the afternoons with her. "Guiding Light" and "Search for Tomorrow" were her favorites.

Mother called most every day. And she came up for a couple of weekends when we would all three move up to the Georgian Terrace and get a room.

There was that one night. I knew there was something special about it when it began, but I didn't know what. Daddy took us out to eat at the Varsity and I had a couple of chili dogs and some

French fries. We went to the Fox Theatre for a movie, and then we went back to the room. They seemed happy together. There was no loud talking and no crying.

When we got back to the hotel room, I jumped into one of the double beds. Usually, when we were together, they took one of the beds and I took the one next to theirs.

But that night, my daddy said, before he turned off the lights, "Come get in bed with us."

I needed no further invitation. I hopped in between my daddy and my mother, and they both put their arms around me.

This was my dream! I had no other. To be with them that way was as sweet a peace as I have ever known. For the first time in a long time, I thought there might be a chance for a reunion.

I said to them, "Why can't it be this way every night?"

I don't think they ever answered me. I guess they really didn't have an easy answer for why it couldn't be either.

Mother went back to Moreland. At the end of the month, Daddy asked me if I were ready to go home. I said I wasn't. He came home from work the next afternoon, and he asked if I wanted to go on a trip. I, of course, was up for anything he suggested.

We caught a bus. We rode to Heflin, Alabama, just across the Georgia line. We stayed with people he knew, an old couple who fawned over me. They fed us, and then Daddy and I went to bed. I had no idea of the adventure upon which I was about to embark.

He had done it a second time. He had taken me and split again. I can't remember how long we were away, and where all we went. We stayed in a different house in a different town most every night.

Occasionally, we would stay in a motel. Daddy didn't go to work, of course, but it never occurred to me at the time where he was getting the money on which we ate and traveled. I know now, however. He was charming it off anybody who would listen to him for five minutes and nobody ever was successful in ignoring him.

We were in a small east Georgia town, Tignal, for a couple of days. Daddy said he knew a man there. The man—I seem to remember he knew Daddy from the army—put us up in his house for several days.

Daddy told the man I needed to have some dental work before school began in the fall. He mentioned he was a bit on the low side as far as cash was concerned, but if the man could advance him a couple of hundred, he would make certain to pay him back as soon as school started and he began a mahvelous new teaching job in God-knows-where. No problem, said the man, handing over the cash. We caught the next Greyhound out of town.

We were in south Georgia for a time. What kept us there for so long, I believe now, was the Georgia-Florida Class D League. I never thought to ask him, but I think Daddy missed coaching.

We hit Tifton and Saturday was spent fighting the mosquitoes in a dark little ballpark watching Tifton play Albany, which is pronounced "All-

banny" by the locals. We later stayed in a hotel in Albany. I remember that one day we went to a movie and saw Walt Disney's *Lady and the Tramp.*

At night, we would go to the ball park, and Daddy would talk to the ball players and the manager. Once, he came back with a T-shirt for me that said ALBANY CARDINALS on the front. We later went to Waycross to see a game and Daddy talked to this man and to that man, and after the game, we boarded the bus with the Waycross team.

"Your daddy," he said to me proudly, "is going to coach for Waycross."

I never knew all the details, but it was something about the team's first-base coach being in the hospital and they had agreed to take on Daddy until he got well.

The next two weeks, I lived out an incredible fantasy. I was with my daddy and my daddy was with a ball team. I remember the Latin ball players chattering nonstop in the back of the bus. Daddy bought me a glove and I played pitch with the players before every ball game. They even let me into a pepper game occasionally.

We ate in greasy diners. I ate hamburgers three meals a day. On the bus rides, I would sit next to Daddy and he would tell army stories.

"I had this center fielder at Benning one time could outrun anything or anybody. In the name of God, was he fast. I called him 'Rabbit.'

"We were playing on the road one night and there was no outfield fence. The lights stopped and then it was just dark back in there for I don't know how far.

"We were leading late in the game and they had the bases loaded with two outs. They had an old boy had already hit two home runs to left. He just hit the ball through the lights and nobody could catch up to it.

"Well, he hit another one toward center. I hollered, 'Go get it, Rabbit!'

"Ol' Rabbit turned and started running. He went clean out of sight past those lights. In a few seconds, he came back, holding the ball up. The umpires had to take his word for it that he caught it, and we won the ball game.

"On the bus ride back home, I said, 'Rabbit, did you really catch that ball?'

"He said, 'No, Skip, but I had done seen that man hit two past the lights, so I stuck another ball in my pocket in case he hit one my way."

The Waycross dream finally ended. We caught a train to Savannah and stayed with more relatives for a few days.

"Everybody is looking for you," they said to Daddy. "They say Christine is wild, she's so worried. They say she's done called in the law to find you."

We immediately got on another train and ended up in Columbia, South Carolina. We passed a department store on the way to a hotel and saw a Davy Crockett buckskin outfit in the window. I asked Daddy if I could have it. He never turned me down.

We went into the store and I tried on the suit while Daddy began talking to the salesperson.

"I'm Major Grizzard," he said. (Major? His last

rank in the army had been captain. But the more I think of it now, "Major" did fit him perfectly. Captains are tall, young straight arrows. Majors, on the other hand, are usually older and wiser, and more jocular, and they command a bit more respect for their age and experience. Daddy did stop promoting himself after Major, however. I never knew him to refer to himself as "General," but, who knows, had he not died so young, he might have made it.)

Daddy went on with his pitch to the salesperson.

"My son and I are just moving into Columbia," he said, "and I haven't had time to open a checking account. Would you be so kind as to take an out-of-town check?"

The salesperson hesitated, so Daddy hit him with more of his charm and not only did he finally cash the check, he cashed it for thirty dollars more than the price of the suit. We were in the money again.

"They have a mahvelous baseball team in this town," Daddy told me. Our first night then we went straight for the Columbia park. This was Class A, Daddy explained, the Sally League.

He went down to the dugout again before the game and called to one of the players and said he was Major Lewis Grizzard of the Waycross Braves. I prepared for more bus rides and hamburgers.

But they didn't have need of a first-base coach in Columbia. We checked out of the hotel the next day. We walked, our suitcases in our hands, to a nearby highway and Daddy introduced me to the art of hitchhiking.

The first driver took us to Aiken, South Carolina, just across the Savannah River from Augusta, Georgia. Then, we got a ride to Thomson, Georgia, and just before night, a man picked us up who was going all the way to Athens. Daddy put a few moves on him, and he invited us to spend the night in his house. The next day he lent Daddy money for our bus fares to Atlanta.

When we got to Atlanta, Daddy called Aunt Rufy to come and get us. She started screaming at Daddy the minute she picked us up. She hadn't stopped when we got to her house.

"In the name of God, Rufy," he said, "won't you please just hush?"

Rufy called my mother. She was there in a couple of hours. She screamed, too.

"I had the law after you!" she roared. Daddy just hung his head.

"You'll never see this child again!" she screamed further.

I started crying.

"I'm sorry, Christine" was Daddy's reply in between screams. "Please don't hate me."

"You've ruined your life, you've ruined my life, and you're not going to ruin this child's!"

She took me home to Moreland. I begged to stay with Daddy. I clung to him, and she had to pull me away.

"I want to stay with my daddy!" I shouted.

"You're coming home," Mother said.

I persisted. Daddy bent down and looked at me.

"Go with your mother, son," he said. And then he hugged me, as was his custom. I wanted to beg Mother to let me stay, but I sensed it was fruitless. My mother always was a woman of resolve.

I think I knew it was over after that. There would be no end to the separation of my mother and my daddy. She would always be in one place and he in another.

On the way home, I said, "You aren't going to make me not see Daddy again, are you?"

She let go of her anger for just a moment.

"Your daddy can't take you away and not let me know where you are again. He shouldn't do that."

That hadn't answered my question.

"We'll see about another visit," she eventually said.

I knew my mother's "we'll-see's" leaned to the positive side, and so I went back to Moreland with at least a glimmer of hope that I would be visiting Daddy again. Mother was quick to anger, but she also was quick to forgive.

I saw Daddy again on Christmas. I spent a weekend with him back in Atlanta. He bought me a new basketball and a hoop. Daddy Bun erected it on the side of his garage when I returned home.

There were no more long stays with Daddy. I would see him a weekend here, and a weekend there.

He went back to Arkansas. He was in Florida. He got a job coaching girls' basketball at a small high school near Augusta.

He would never stay anywhere for very long. There always would be a bad check to come looking for him. Or he would go off on a bender. He was never any sort of a drinker but a bender drinker. He would go weeks without a drop, but sooner or later, he would be at the bottom of a number of bottles in some hotel or motel room. He'd call sometimes when he was drunk, and I could tell the difference in him. He would cry and make me promises and he would say how much he loved my mother, and then she would get on the phone with him and tell him not to call back until he was sober.

My mother's brother Johnny was a doctor. He ran the medical ward at the State Hospital in Milledgeville, a home for the mentally disturbed.

Uncle Johnny convinced Daddy at one point he could help him. Daddy checked into the hospital and Uncle Johnny spent a long time talking to him.

Uncle Johnny told Mother, "Lewis lives in a make-believe world. He will not accept what has happened to him. He lives in a fantasy that he has retired from the army. He introduced himself to some of the doctors as Major Grizzard.

"I think he really believes he is going to straighten himself out. He believes you are coming back to him. I think he goes on those benders when he has doses of reality. If he promises you the moon, I think he has every intention of carrying it out. What we have to convince him of is that he is a sick man, and he must deal with reality without drinking to run away."

My mother asked Uncle Johnny if Daddy could ever be violent.

"Not a chance," he answered.

She asked if Uncle Johnny thought he ever could "straighten himself out" (that phrase again).

"It would take a long, long time," Uncle Johnny answered.

I had listened to their conversation through a closed door. More hope flew from me. My daddy was in Milledgeville in what the kids called the "nut house," and Uncle Johnny said he wouldn't get better for a long, long time.

Daddy left the hospital in Milledgeville when he finally got tired of it or the urge to move on became too strong to fight.

He called one night soon afterward and said he would be driving back through Moreland the next day on his way to Columbus. He said the army wanted to talk to him about getting his records changed. The reality was, of course, that the army wouldn't do anything of the kind, but Daddy dreamed on.

He said he would meet us at the fork of Highways 27 and 29, at Steve Smith's truck stop. He said to meet him at four.

We stayed until past nine. He never showed. Instead, he sent a money order for twenty dollars two weeks later. Another time, he called and asked Mother to meet him again in Griffin. We drove over Friday afternoon to the Peter Pan Motel. He never came that night, either.

The two disappointments were daggers. Daddy had the power to swing my moods from high ecstasy to the darkest and most hopeless of abysses. But I couldn't let go of him, no matter what he did to me. I forgave everything. I never could understand why everybody else wouldn't do the same.

I lived on memories. My grandfather had a stand of scuppernong vines behind his garage. It was dark and cool under those vines. I would go there alone, lie on my back, pick and eat scuppernongs, relive those memories, and daydream about making others.

I never saw it coming, of course. The thing hit me blindside. If I didn't already have enough to trouble me. I was about to have more. A man asked my mother for a date.

CHAPTER
10

IT NEVER OCCURRED TO ME THAT EITHER OF MY PARENTS would marry again. Mother first went out with an ambulance driver who showed up to take her out in his ambulance.

He tried to make friends with me, asking if I would like to hear his siren.

"I'd like to hear it on the way out of here," I said.

Later, he tried to make friends again by taking me along on a date with my mother. We went to the Alamo Theatre, in Newnan, where there was a documentary about Bonnie and Clyde. Outside the theater, they even had the actual car in which Bonnie and Clyde had been blown to bits.

I might have had a nice time had it not been for the fact one of my friends spotted me getting out of an ambulance with my mother and her date.

"Who's that man?" he asked me.

"I forget his name," I said.

"What are you doing in an ambulance?" he went on.

I was terribly embarrassed for one of my friends to see my mother out with a man, not to mention the fact I was riding in what was known at that time as a "meat wagon."

I made up this wild story that Mother and I were driving to see the movie, and we had this wreck and the ambulance came to take us to the hospital, but we got a lot better on the way and decided to see a movie instead. I knew I was hovering near the bounds of my credibility, but it was better than admitting the truth.

By the way, the movie stunk, and I don't think that was Bonnie and Clyde's real car, and the ambulance driver wore white socks with his blue suit. The night was a total loss.

I was jealous of my mother. The fact she was seeing other men made my hopes of parental reconciliation grow dimmer still.

Mother went to a dance in Newnan with my aunt and uncle, who were visiting, and she met a man named H.B. Atkinson, an appliance salesman.

They were married October 25, 1956, five days past my tenth birthday. I was against the marriage, and I said so in a number of different ways, such as throwing temper tantrums and trying to kick my mother's fiancé in the shins.

They ignored me the best they could and got married anyway.

It was only after H.B. proposed to my mother and she accepted that she went ahead and got a divorce from Daddy. I knew a little about divorce and I asked an older cousin if people got divorced and they had a child, could the child decide which parent he wanted to live with. She said that was correct.

I announced to Mother I was going to live with Daddy.

"You want to leave me?" she asked.

"You got what's-his-name," I said, or something to that effect.

"You'll get used to H.B.," she went on.

No, I won't, I thought to myself, and I decided at that point to make H.B.'s life miserable. I also found out my cousin didn't know anything about divorce. Kids don't have anything to say about which parent they want to live with until they're eighteen or something like that. I faced eight long years before I could go live with Daddy.

H.B. made a serious mistake with me soon after he and Mother married. He decided I needed some chores to do because, as he stated his case, when he was my age, he was working eighteen hours a day in the tobacco field. Adults always tell children things like that—"I had to walk eight miles barefoot through the snow to go to school"—to make them feel guilty.

It didn't work on me. I didn't care how long he had labored when he was my age. Besides, that was back when there wasn't anything else to do but work. Now we had television and bicycles and ball games and air rifles and all sorts of modern conveniences to occupy our time.

I'm not sure, but I think H.B. wanted to make a farmer out of me. He planted a garden and insisted I help in such agricultural endeavors as tying bean stalks to poles, bending over to pick up potatoes out of the just-plowed ground, and hoeing weeds. He even bought me my own hoe.

I would do anything to get out of such work. One day, I couldn't work because I had a wart or mole. Another time, I said I had seen a snake in the garden and it would be cruel and unusual punishment to send a small child into where there are snakes.

H.B. was a stubborn man. He didn't care if I got snakebite or not, he sent me out there with nothing to fight off snakes but my stupid hoe.

H.B. was trying to become a father replacement to me. But I didn't want one. My resentment toward him grew each day we lived together. Rather than a replacement, I saw him as an intruder. What was he doing sleeping with my mother? What was he doing bossing me around? He was a big man, and I feared what might happen if one day he got his fill of my smart aleckness. But I risked it. He had to know he wasn't my daddy and I would never accept him as my daddy. No matter who my mother had married, I still would have reacted to any sort of man the same way.

But to make matters worse, there couldn't have been a more dichotomous pair, H.B. and Daddy. H.B. didn't seem to know one end of a baseball bat from the other. He probably didn't even know the infield fly rule and never once in conversation had he ever mentioned two of my biggest heroes, Duke Snider and Gil Hodges of the Dodgers.

He was quiet. He drank a little beer, but I never

saw him go to the bathroom outside, and we had twelve acres on which to go.

I felt like he picked on me.

"Don't smack while you're eating," he would say at the supper table.

"Don't walk with your shoulders slouched."

"Quit making motorboat sounds in your soup."

"Put a handkerchief over your nose and mouth when you sneeze."

"Help your mother bring in the groceries."

"Don't come in the bedroom before you knock."

I can look back now and agree I needed a bit of discipline in my life, but the more H.B. came down on me, the more I rebelled.

The Boy Scouts had a father-son dinner at the school. I didn't want to go because I was still embarrassed my mother was married to somebody besides my father. Divorce at that time was not yet in the epidemic stage, especially in a quiet, down-the-straight-and-narrow village like Moreland.

We went, H.B. and I, to the father-son dinner and things were going along very well until he insisted I eat my little green English peas. We had turkey and dressing and rolls with lots of butter and pound cake, and I ate all that, but I didn't eat my English peas because I was born hating English peas and I still hate them.

People were leaving the dinner.

"You've got to eat your English peas before we can go," H.B. said to me.

Had the man lost his mind?

"I don't like English peas," I said.

"How do you know?" H.B. asked. "You haven't tried them."

"I tried them a long time ago and I got sick."

"English peas won't make you sick. Eat them."

"I'm not eating them."

"Yes, you are. We're not leaving until you eat the peas."

I could have waited him out, and I considered that. Not only did I hate the peas, but there was a matter of principle here. Nobody, I decided, should have the right to make another person eat English peas if he didn't want to. I think that was one of the things that started the American Revolution.

I could have just sat there, refusing to eat the peas until morning came and then H.B. would have to go to work, and I still wouldn't have eaten the peas.

I changed my mind, however, when H.B. explained it to me like this: "Either eat the peas or I'm going to whip you in front of all your friends."

A fate worse than death, that. A fate worse than eating a few English peas, as well. I ate the peas, but I resented every one of them.

Daddy wouldn't have made me eat the peas, I thought to myself before going to sleep that night. He probably wouldn't have eaten his.

"In the name of God," he would have said, "these English peas are awful."

I mentioned that to my mother the next day.

"Daddy wouldn't have made me eat the peas," I said.

She took H.B.'s side.

"He's just trying to teach you that you shouldn't waste food," she said.

I still don't believe that. What I believe is, he made me eat the peas to prove to me the fact he was now squarely in charge of my life and I had better not have any ideas otherwise.

I still made his life miserable every chance I got. I hoed as slowly as I could. I continued to smack my food at the supper table, as loudly as possible.

"A cow doesn't make that much noise when she eats," H.B. said.

"Moo," was my clever response.

I got a whipping for that clever response, but when one is fighting a guerrilla war against his stepfather, one has to expect to take a few lumps every now and then.

We had what could be described as a major confrontation our first Christmas together. Daddy had called and asked if I could come and see him in Atlanta for a few days during the Christmas holidays.

No problem, I figured. I mentioned it to Mother.

"I think H.B. wants you to go with us to visit his family in South Carolina," she said.

I thought she misunderstood what I said, so I repeated it for her.

"Daddy wants me to come see him for Christmas."

"You'll have to ask H.B.," she said.

I was appalled. Ask H.B. if I could go see my daddy? Wasn't it enough that I had to give up my place next to my mother in bed and sleep all alone on a couch? Wasn't it enough that I put up with eating English peas and all the *do's* and *don't's* and *stop's* and *quit's* and went out and slaved in the fields when I could have been watching a ball game on television?

This was a horrible affront. I hadn't seen Daddy in six months and now this man was going to deny my seeing him for Christmas?

"H.B.," I said carefully after I found him outside washing his car. "I want to go see Daddy for Christmas."

"I want you to go to South Carolina with me and your mother. I want you to meet my people," he said.

I tried to reason with him.

"I'm not going to South Carolina and I'm not meeting with your folks. I'm going to see my daddy."

"No, you're going with me and your mother," he reasoned back.

I pitched what my grandmother had once called a "running fit." I began to run in no particular direction, crying as loudly as I could. One might exhibit the same behavior after just being stung by a large number of bees.

I stopped just long enough to pound my fists against the ground. I cursed at the sky and covered my face with my hands in utter anguish. I ran into the house and found my mother and I said, "I hate H.B.! I hate him!"

"You shouldn't say you hate people," she replied.

"I hate his guts!" I said.

"Go out there and apologize to him for saying that."

"No."

"Go."

"No."

"Young man, you march right out there and tell H.B. you are sorry for saying you hate him."

I walked the long mile back outside where H.B. continued to wash his car.

"Mother said for me to say I'm sorry I said I hated you," I managed to force out of my tormented innards.

"Go wash your face," said H.B.

I called Daddy back the next day and told him of what had befallen me.

"Put your mother on the phone," he said.

Mother listened to what he had to say and then told him the matter was closed.

I got back on the phone and sobbed. Daddy said if Mother wouldn't allow me to come see him, there was nothing he could do.

I said I would run away.

"Just lay low, son," he said. "I'll see you right after Christmas."

I went to South Carolina with Mother and H.B. and that's where I spent Christmas, with people I never had seen before. I was fairly irritable the entire time I was there. We went to visit Aunt So-and-so and Cousin Whatever and I was as unpleasant as I could be without bringing down any physical wrath on myself.

We were there a week. It was an imprisonment. Mother was no help. She was trying to make a good impression on her new in-laws, I suppose. In retrospect, they were very nice people and they treated me kindly, but it wouldn't have mattered how they treated me. I was determined to be miserable and I did a magnificent job at it.

H.B. and I were rarely cordial after that. He was my sworn enemy. Mother became referee. When she took H.B.'s side, I pouted. When she took mine, he would go to the Moose Club in Newnan and drink beer.

When I was twelve, Daddy married again. He married Betty Cawthon, and they moved into her house in the Atlanta suburb of East Point.

Betty was no threat to me. I liked her as a matter of fact, and I liked the idea that Daddy had a new home. At least now I would know where he was. Maybe now he would settle down and *straighten himself out.*

Betty had a son. His name was Bob Hanson. He was twenty-two when Daddy and Betty got married. He had a wife and two children, and I had a new stepbrother.

Bob and my daddy became very close. I began to make regular visits to see Daddy and Betty, and I took to Bob immediately. He and Daddy were very much alike, it seemed to me.

They were both big men with robust appetites and senses of humor. Bob would tell a joke and Daddy would throw his head back and laugh and say, "Roh-but, Roh-but, Roh-but, what a mahvelous story."

Betty doted on Daddy. I hated it when H.B. and Mother got chummy with each other, but this was different. The double standard came from the fact that if Betty were good to Daddy, he would stay with her and that would afford me many more opportunities to be with him.

I took the bus up to see them on various weekends. Betty would cook supper. She was a wonderful cook. Then Daddy and Bob and me would be off to a ball game or a movie. Daddy and Bob were splendid together, and what jealousy I felt came from the fact Bob could be with him anytime he pleased, and I couldn't.

But those weekends were magnificent, and on Sunday nights when they ended, I was crushed I had to leave.

Betty drove us to the bus station in East Point. She drove, I sat in the middle, and Daddy sat beside me.

"I always know," Betty said as we were preparing to leave for the station, "when it's almost time for you to go. You start sighing."

As elated as I would feel on Fridays when I arrived, it was no comparison to the depression I felt upon leaving. And it still showed at home.

I came home those Sunday nights bitterly disappointed my visit with Daddy and Betty was over.

I sulked. I disobeyed. I sassed. Even Daddy Bun, gentle as he was, called me down one evening at the supper table when I said something back to Mother.

"You'd better watch your step, young man," Mother said. "If you don't come back here in a better mood, H.B. may not let you go visit anymore."

That would have annihilated me. I did attempt some alteration of my behavior after that. Nothing was worth the price of being kept from Betty and Daddy and Bob.

But nothing seemed to stay on any sort of consistent path for me. Daddy got a job (a "mahvelous" one) in Camden, South Carolina, working as the food manager in a hospital. He and Betty moved from East Point. I still managed a couple of visits, but they did not come nearly as frequently as before the move. I missed Bob, too. He soon moved himself to take a new job in Birmingham.

Daddy and Betty stayed in South Carolina a year. They might have stayed longer, but one day, Daddy took off on a bender to God-knows-where and lost his job.

Betty called me in Moreland to see if I had heard from him. I hadn't. She said she was going to Bob's in Birmingham in the meantime.

I lost track of Bob and Betty—and Daddy—for maybe six months after that. Then, as was his custom, Daddy called from out of the blue.

"Where are you?" I asked.

"I have this mahvelous new job in Birmingham," he said. "I'm managing a country club."

He said he would send me bus fare so I could come and visit. He said he and Betty were together and were living with Bob. The thought of a reunion with the three of them was thrilling.

I flagged the bus to Atlanta, where I had to make a change to another bus for Birmingham.

The bus was to arrive in Birmingham at 8:00 P.M. Friday night. Daddy was to meet me.

But when I got off the bus, Daddy wasn't there. He had never done this before. He had never

asked me to visit him and then not shown up. I was
fifteen, and I was frightened. I sat down in the waiting room and waited.

I was there a half hour. I had five dollars. I
thought of calling home, but that would just make
it more difficult the next time I wanted to be with
Daddy.

A man walked over to me and asked if my name
was Lewis *Griz*-zerd (the unacceptable pronunciation).

"Lewis Griz-*zard,*" I corrected him.

"Your daddy sent me to get you in my cab."

"Why isn't he here?" I asked.

"I don't know," said the driver. "Dispatch just
said your daddy called and wanted you picked up
at the bus station."

I got into the cab. I had no idea where we were
going. Where we were going turned out to be a
country club on the east side of Birmingham.

I was hoping Daddy wasn't drunk. He was. I
didn't like the way he smelled when he was drunk.
Daddy paid the driver.

"What are you doing here?" I asked him.

"I'm the manager here," his thick tongue said.
"I'm taking care of the club while it's closed for a
week."

He was in a small house behind the main club
building. There was a bed inside and a chair. That
was all.

I was angry at him. I had looked forward to the
visit, I wanted to say, and I find this. But I didn't
tell him. I never told Daddy when I was angry at
him.

He poured a glassful of whiskey and then he drank it down. He poured another. Then he stretched out on the bed and went to sleep.

There was only one bed. I had to sleep next to him. That close, the smell was even worse. For the first time in my life, I wanted to be somewhere else besides with my daddy.

He awakened before I did. When I opened my eyes, he was sitting in the chair, and he was drinking again. It was Saturday morning. I was supposed to catch the bus back to Moreland Sunday. I began to worry how I would get back to the Birmingham bus station if he never sobered up enough to drive. There was a car parked in front of the house, but I didn't know if it was his, or, if it was, whether he'd even be able to drive.

I went exploring. Among other things, I was looking for breakfast. I went inside the main club building. It was deserted. I walked into a room that had more whiskey bottles than I had ever seen. Somebody had made the crucial error of thinking they could leave Daddy alone with a fully stocked bar and get away with it. There was enough booze there to get everybody in east Birmingham knee walking.

I found the kitchen. In the icebox was some milk. I found cereal in a cupboard and had breakfast. When I returned to the house, Daddy was back asleep.

The phone rang. I answered it.

"Who is this?" the voice on the other end said.

I said my name.

"I don't believe it," the voice said. "This is Bob."

I didn't believe it, either.

"Where is Lewis?" he asked.

"Right here."

"Is he drunk?"

"Very."

"Stay right there," Bob urged. "I'm coming to get you."

He told me the entire story when he arrived. Daddy just kept right on sleeping.

After Daddy lost his job in South Carolina, Bob had invited his mother and Daddy to move in with him in Birmingham.

"I hoped if Lewis lived with me, maybe I could keep him off the bottle," Bob said.

Daddy eventually wound up with the job at the country club.

"He told me it was a *mahvelous* job," Bob said.

A couple of days before, however, Daddy had not come home from work. Bob said he called him at the club and he sounded fine. Then he'd tried to call him a couple of more times, but Daddy hadn't answered the phone. Bob thought he had left town.

"I'll take you home and get you something to eat," Bob said. "We'll look after your daddy later."

We left him there, comatose.

Bob was fuming.

"How in the hell can he have you come over here, knowing what kind of shape he was going to be in?" he asked. He must have been asking himself because I certainly had no answer.

We drove back to Bob's house, where I had lunch and a shower. Bob went to his office for a couple of hours. He said Betty had gone back to her house in East Point after Daddy had joined the missing.

"Let's go get him," Bob said.

Daddy wasn't there when we returned to the club.

"Where on earth could a man in his shape go?" Bob wondered.

The car was still there. We surmised he had taken a cab somewhere.

"I'll bet I know where he is," Bob said. "Everytime he gets in this shape, he winds up at the nearest motel."

The nearest motel was the Motel Birmingham. Bob went in and asked if there was a Lewis Grizzard registered there.

"Big guy, drunk?" the clerk asked.

The man gave Bob a key to Daddy's room. He was comatose again. A half-empty bottle of bourbon and a glass were on the dresser next to the bed.

The phone rang. It was the clerk at the front desk.

"Who's going to pay his bill?" the clerk asked Bob.

"You checked him in without an advance payment," Bob said. "It's your problem."

"Get him out of here right now, or I'm calling the police."

"If you call the police, you aren't ever going to get paid," Bob said. "Now, if you will just be the slightest bit patient and give me some time, maybe I can get him out of here, and I'll pay the bill."

Bob hung up.

Daddy was in his shorts and T-shirt. He was snoring loudly.

Bob tried shaking him. Nothing.

He sent me out to get a bucket of ice. Bob wrapped the ice in a towel, then wet down the towel with cold water.

He pulled up Daddy's T-shirt and laid the ice and wet towel on his stomach. He didn't even flinch.

We tried more ice and more wet towels. We continued shaking and screaming. A half hour later, we got a few sounds, and then he opened his eyes.

"Roh-but, Roh-but, Roh-but," he said.

"Don't 'Roh-but' me, Lewis," Bob shot back. "We've got to get you out of here before the police come."

Bob and I pulled him up on his feet.

"Don't hate me, Roh-but," Daddy said.

"I don't hate you, Lewis," Bob replied. "I don't like you very much right now, but I don't hate you."

We dressed him and held on to him as he staggered toward Bob's car. Bob paid the room clerk.

"It just occurred to me," Bob said when he got back into the car. "What are we going to do with him now? I can't take him back to my house in this shape. And I don't want to take him back to Mother's in East Point. She doesn't need this."

We started driving around Birmingham as Bob tried to devise some sort of plan. Daddy had gone back to sleep in the backseat.

"There's only one thing to do with him," Bob said, "and that's take him to your Aunt Rufy's in Atlanta."

It was a three-hour drive. We stopped once for a hamburger. Daddy sat up in the backseat.

"You want something to eat, Lewis?" Bob asked.

"I need a little drink, *Roh*-but," Daddy said.

"That's the last thing you need."

"Don't hate me, Roh-but."

He lay back down and went back to sleep.

He was in a fair condition when we drove up to his sister Rufy's house. He begged Bob to forgive him.

"Don't worry about me forgiving you," Bob said. "Worry about your son forgiving you."

Daddy turned to me.

"Will you please pardon me?" he asked.

I had never seen him appear so weak. Instead of the booming voice, I was hearing what was almost a whine.

"I forgive you," I said. I did, eventually, of course. But not at that very moment. He was too drunk to pick me up at the bus station, and he had ruined what I hoped would be a great weekend with him. I felt what Bob felt; I didn't hate Daddy, but at that moment, I don't think I liked him very much.

Aunt Rufy was much more direct about her feelings.

"Lewis, look what an awful mess you have made of yourself," she said. "And I can't believe you would allow yourself to get into this kind of shape with your own son coming to visit you."

"Don't hate me," Daddy pleaded.

"I don't know why I shouldn't," Aunt Rufy said.

I just sat there and listened. When Rufy finished

her salvoes, Daddy was a man defeated. Rufy put him to bed.

"Don't tell Mother he did this," I said to her.

"She ought to know," she said back.

"It will just make her worry," I went on.

"I don't know what's going to happen to your daddy. It's a shame what he's done to himself."

I shrugged my shoulders. I didn't know what was going to happen to him, either.

Daddy was better Sunday morning. He shaved with Uncle Harry's razor and borrowed one of Uncle Harry's shirts to wear.

He never apologized to me. I think to have done so would have been to admit to a reality he had no intention of facing. Aunt Rufy took us downtown to see a movie. Afterward, we walked over to the Greyhound station to catch my bus home.

He hugged and kissed me before I stepped on the bus.

"I love you, son," he said.

"I love you too, Daddy," I said.

That wasn't what I wanted to say. I wanted for once to tell him I was angry with him, that I was disappointed, that I had to go back to Moreland not knowing when or where I would see him next.

My mother asked if I had enjoyed the trip to Birmingham.

I said it was *mahvelous.*

CHAPTER
11

I LOOKED FOR MY DADDY, OR PARTS OF MY DADDY, IN OTHER men when I was a child, and I continued that practice on into adulthood. I never accepted anyone as Daddy's total replacement, but as I began to realize my own father never would play a full-time role in my life, I attempted to fill the voids he had left by seeking out men who reminded me of different portions of his personality.

There was a great man in Moreland when I was growing up. His name was Red Murphy. He was the postmaster in the tiny, white-framed Moreland post office on what we called "the square," which had a store and the post office and the knitting mill and the railroad tracks and an abandoned building that once had been a bank, on another side, and the Methodist Church, all of which surrounded a vacant lot in the middle.

Mr. Red was a happy, red-faced man with a

high-pitched voice. He had a pony and a wagon and on Sunday afternoons, he would ride around Moreland and take children on rides.

He also was one of the Boy Scout leaders. He taught me how to tie the knots it was necessary for me to learn to get my Tenderfoot ranking. You don't easily forget a man who played such a role in your development into a well-rounded individual.

Mr. Red, as the children called him, had three children. Mike was my age. Danny was older. Then there was a baby daughter, Molly. Mr. Red had a farm a half mile from my house, and down in those woods of his, Mike and I and our other friends partook of every pleasure available in the 1950s for rural children.

We dammed the creek a thousand times. We built a tree house and spent the night in it. We made cigarettes out of what we called "rabbit tobacco" and we rolled it with paper we tore out of the Sears and Roebuck catalog. As long as you didn't inhale, smoking rabbit tobacco was at least a slightly pleasant experience.

We had rat killings. I have done many enjoyable things since I was a kid in Moreland, but few have held the excitement of a rat killing at Mr. Red Murphy's.

Mr. Red had a barn where he stored his corn. Rats like corn. I'm not certain exactly why, but rats like corn.

The best time to hold a rat killing is at night. The idea is to slip quietly into the barn where the corn is stored. Listen and you can hear the rats gnawing away at the corn.

This thing should have been on "Wide World of Sports" or something like that. It had to be more interesting than those people who are always diving off those cliffs in Mexico.

One person goes over to the light switch in the barn. When he hits the lights, it momentarily blinds the rats. In those precious few seconds the rats are blinded, they are sitting ducks—or rats—for .22 rifle fire.

Rat killing probably sounds a lot like the St. Valentine's Day Massacre. Blam! Blam! Blam! As fast as we could deliver them, the volleys poured in against the rats. It was no extraordinary event when we managed to send forty-five or fifty rats home to the Lord in one evening. The Murphys' grateful cats took care of most of the dead rats and the Murphys, unlike other local farmers, normally lost very little of their corn to the dreaded rodents.

Mr. Red had a heart attack and died when he was still a relatively young man. At the funeral, the preacher said, "Red's family has lost a wonderful, loving husband and father. Moreland has lost a great citizen. Moreland's children have lost their best friend."

I was fourteen when Mr. Red died. I remember looking at my friend Mike, Red's son, at the funeral. He looked stunned. There were no tears, just a blank stare.

I tried to imagine what it would be like if my daddy died. I couldn't imagine it. The thought was much too painful, too unthinkable.

I remembered that soon after Daddy came back from Korea, he and Mother talked about the fact he had a blood clot. I didn't know what that was, of course, but they seemed concerned and some of that anxiety naturally filtered down to me.

But my daddy had lived through Korea, I said to myself, and nothing could happen to him now. Children are much more able to comfort themselves with strained logic than are adults.

I did feel a loss when Mr. Red died. Mike and I used to walk home from grammar school together. I enjoyed telling him about my daddy, whom I always characterized as nothing less than a heroic superman. Mike always listened to me. He was a nice outlet.

"My daddy was a basketball player," I would say to Mike.

"Mine, too."

"Mine was the one who shot from outside."

"My daddy was a jumping center."

"Could your daddy shoot from outside?"

"I guess."

"My daddy never missed from the outside. Once, he scored fifty points in a game."

"Fifty?"

"Yeah," I would reply, knowing I had the conversation well in hand at that point. "And after he did that, he went out and showed all his soldiers how to fight a war."

If children had said such back then, I am certain Mike would have said, "Awesome."

I always have been drawn to strong men, whose courage and knowledge and abilities in manly practices could never be doubted. What I was doing was attempting to fill that unending sense of emptiness

with which a son is left when there is no father to
forge him security and contentment.

Bobby Entrekin's daddy knew more about sports
than any other man in town. He was the one who
explained the infield fly rule to me. He showed me
how to choke up on a bat and how to run on my
toes so my eyes wouldn't jiggle when I chased a fly
ball.

Dudley Stamps's daddy ran a store. He smoked
big cigars and let Dudley drive me around in the
woods in his truck when we were years from a legal
driver's license.

Eddie Estes's daddy built him a basketball goal
and one day when Eddie and I were playing, he
showed us how to shoot hook shots.

Charlie Bohannon was Scoutmaster. Once I got
mad at something or other at a Scout meeting and
ran home in tears. I went and hid in my bed. After
the Scout meeting, Charlie came over to my house. I
thought he was going to say something derogatory
about me to Mother and H.B. I could hear him talking. All he talked about was what a good Scout I
was and how he thought one day I would be an
Eagle. When Charlie died, I remembered that incident. I wish I had thought of thanking him for not
ratting on me.

Pete Moore organized a baseball team for boys in
Moreland. He managed to get somebody to donate
balls and bats. The second year we played, we even
got uniforms.

He was a big man like Daddy. He had black,
curly hair and he had hams for hands. Somebody
said he used to be a catcher. We played our games

against neighboring towns' teams behind the Moreland school building. When I pitched a no-hitter, he let me keep the game ball. When he talked to me during a game or during practice, he always put his arm around me.

I let him down only once. We were playing Arnco-Sargent from the other side of the county, and I was in center field. We led 6–5. Arnco-Sargent had runners at second and third and two out in the last inning.

The batter hit a looping fly ball toward me. I had momentarily lost interest in the game and was watching a teenage girl in tight shorts who was standing behind the visitor's bench when the ball was hit.

I got a late start and the ball got by me. Two runs were scored and we lost 7–6.

"Grizzard cost us the game," one of my teammates said to Mr. Pete when we came off the field. I was terribly embarrassed.

Mr. Pete put that arm around me and said, "Why don't you ride home with me and I'll get Sarah [his wife] to fix you some country steak and mashed potatoes?"

He never once mentioned my misplay. I ate country-fried steak and mashed potatoes until I was sick.

Bobby Norton, who later became a minister, was my seventh-grade basketball coach and homeroom teacher. He used to take me to Atlanta with him to see the Crackers play. He bought me vanilla custard ice cream at the ballpark like my daddy did. There

was this little girl in the seventh grade who was
ugly and ran her mouth all the time.

He was talking to some of the boys one day and
somebody said something unflattering about this
particular girl and Mr. Norton said, "Boys, you're
going to be surprised because when she gets a little
older, she's going to be a knockout and you'll all
want her for a girlfriend."

I didn't believe him at the time, but he was absolutely right. I married her when she was nineteen.

Ronnie Jenkins's daddy, Mr. Bob, was a riot. He
was the postmaster at Grantville, four miles down
the road. When he retired, he entertained himself
by entertaining Ronnie and me with wonderfully
ribald stories from his youth.

We would sit out in the yard with him on hot
days and he would call out to his wife, "Rachel,
bring me another Ancient Age and Coke, and don't
make this one so strong. Leave out some of that
Coke."

It was Mr. Bob Jenkins who probably saved both
his son's life and mine. When we were old enough
to drive, we immediately turned to spending much
of our spare time drinking beer. The normal proce-
dure was to find a curb boy we could bribe into
bringing a six-pack to our car.

"You boys been drinking beer?" Mr. Bob asked
us one night when Ronnie and I arrived home. He
was our friend. We admitted it.

"I tell you what I want you boys to do," he said.
"When you want to drink some beer, I want you to
bring it here to the house and drink it with me.

That way you won't be out driving around in a car and I'll have somebody to talk to."

Danny Thompson's daddy took Danny and me to a square dance once. We met these two girls and Danny's daddy let us take them out to his car and kiss on them until he was ready to leave the square dance. He was a kind man.

I often felt jealous of my friends, that they had fathers and that I had none. Even at a young age, I could sense how other children took their fathers for granted. I was too young to know to tell them of their great fortune.

At some time or other, I coveted most all my friends' fathers. I went to sleep at night with fantasies that by some strange miracle, I suddenly would be another boy, and I would still have the same mother, but that she would be married to this man or to that man who would be my real daddy, and I would know what it is like to have a daddy who never went away. It wasn't a mean fantasy. I didn't want anybody else to lose a father so that I could have one. I just wanted that feeling again, the one I felt the night I slept between both my parents, and I wanted it not for just one night or one week or even the year. I wanted it with no end to it. It seemed others had it that way. I just wanted my piece of the dream.

Such a desire, one whose strength probably is immeasurable, does not readily disappear.

I moved away from home, away from my friends and their fathers, but I never moved away from wanting and seeking and needing the strong influence of an older and wiser and stronger male. It didn't even stop when Daddy died. As a matter of fact, it got stronger, if anything.

I have been married and divorced three times. There were three fathers-in-law to whom I was drawn in one way or the other. The first was a quiet man, a man with an unending patience, who used to take me fishing. We would go off for days together and it was like being back on the creek with Daddy Bun. He taught me to jug fish, my first father-in-law. You take empty jugs and tie a line and a hook to them and then bait the hook. Then, you sit quietly in your boat amidst all the jugs. When a jug starts bobbing up and down, there is a fish on the other end. We once caught forty-five catfish in an hour jug fishing.

When I was on the verge of losing his daughter because of some rather selfish tendencies I exhibited, I called my first father-in-law and I asked him to please ask her to forgive me.

He said he would, and I am certain he did. She never did forgive me, by the way, but at least he cared enough for me to be my hole card, albeit a losing one.

My second father-in-law had a deep voice like my father's. He told a funny story every now and then, too. When I lost his daughter, I knew it wouldn't do any good to call him. When women make up their minds to go, they go. I learned that the first time.

My third father-in-law was much different from the first two. He was a man of the world, a tycoon of sorts. He had his own boat. We played a lot of backgammon together. He was a good player. Once he even invited me to a party he was giving in New York.

He was a very opinionated man. I think he liked me more than he did his other sons-in-law because I never argued with him. I knew to do so would be fruitless.

The man to whom I owe the most is Jim Minter. His name appears on the dedication page of this book. He is not old enough to be my father, and we have the closeness of friends, more than anything else, but his influence upon my life has been great. And I am better for that.

Jim Minter, who lives in Fayette County, Georgia, is editor of the *Atlanta Constitution* and the *Atlanta Journal.* I knew of him when I was a child when he was a sportswriter for the *Journal.* He used to appear on an Atlanta television show called "Football Review" where Atlanta sportswriters discussed the college games they had covered the day before.

Since I was old enough to read box scores, I wanted to be a sportswriter. What I had in mind was covering minor league baseball and riding trains. I was in love with both. Sadly, by the time I was old enough to become a sportswriter, both minor league baseball and trains were gone. But that is another story.

Jim Minter hired me as a sportswriter for the *Journal* when I was twenty-one and just out of the University of Georgia. I have already mentioned that problems with my heart kept me from Vietnam.

I worked for a local newspaper in Athens, where the university is located. How Jim found out about me is he asked the Georgia basketball coach who was the worst young sportswriter in town. The coach named me because I was usually critical of whatever he or his team did.

That was at the beginning of the no-cheering-in-the-pressbox era of sports journalism. Homers were going out. Young bucks with jaundiced eyes were coming in. Minter found me covering a Georgia baseball game one day.

He sat down beside me in the press box. I didn't dare speak before I was spoken to. He wore a pair of sunglasses and clenched a cigar in the right side of his mouth.

We sat there like that, not speaking, for two full innings. Then, without introducing himself—which, of course, was totally unnecessary—he spoke.

"How would you like to go to work for us?" he asked me.

The words came as a lightning bolt from some unseen place in the sky.

How would I like to come to work for you? How would I like to sleep with Dorothy Malone? Sing with Elvis? Catch a pass from Johnny Unitas? My lifetime dream was to be a sportswriter for the *Atlanta Journal,* and this man had just fulfilled it.

I took the job. It paid $160 a week, the most money in the world.

At this writing, nearly twenty years later, Jim Minter has hired me four times at the Atlanta newspapers. The second time was after I quit the *Journal* (he had left earlier to become managing editor of the morning *Constitution)* to follow the silly notion I could make a living as a free-lance writer.

Maybe I could do that now, but not back then. When it didn't work out, Jim found me a spot on the *Constitution.*

A few years later, I quit again to take a job as sports editor of the *Chicago Sun-Times.* The job was fine. Chicago wasn't. I was cold and I was lonely and another man's daughter had decided to move on.

So Jim hired me again. An hour later, however, I changed my mind and turned him down. I had another silly notion that quitting Chicago at that point would be a sign of weakness.

A year later, I didn't care. The newspaper business was changing. They had begun putting carpet on newsroom floors. Some sort of machine where you wrote on a television set was replacing typewriters. What sports editors did was worry about the budget, go to meetings, and fight the union.

I called Jim and told him I wanted to become a writer after ten years as an editor.

"I can't pay you what you're making in Chicago," he said to me.

"I'll work nights in a convenience store," I said.

A week later, I had a job writing a sports column for the *Atlanta Constitution.*

Jim Minter is now a legend at the Atlanta newspapers. There are those who do not like him. There are those, I am certain, who hate him. That is because he is the toughest man in the valley. As another Minterphile once put it, "He is the only man I know who always does the right thing no matter how much it hurts him or somebody else."

There is no way to know Jim Minter and not

have a strong feeling about him. Those who hate him probably do so with a passion. Those of us who love him—and I do love him—love him unconditionally. I saw a religious bumper sticker once that said, "God said it, I believe it. That settles it."

If Minter said it, I believe it. And that settles it.

He is a small man, a quiet man. He will loosen a bit at times, but even then he maintains a guarded posture, which is to say he'll have a couple of Scotches and tell a joke, but he won't loosen his tie. And if his wife says it is time to go home, he goes home.

When *Atlanta Constitution* editor Reg Murphy was kidnapped, the kidnapper demanded $800,000 in cash be delivered to him at a remote site by someone driving an open vehicle.

Minter, then managing editor and not always on the best of terms with Murphy, volunteered to go. He put on a ski mask to guard against the cold and drove out to meet the kidnapper in a jeep with the $800,000. When Minter came back safely and Murphy was freed, somebody at the *Constitution* wrote a story about how worried the staff was about Minter.

"All managing editors are sons of bitches," went one line, "but he was *our* son of a bitch."

Somebody asked Minter later what it felt like leaving the *Journal-Constitution* building with $800,000 of the company's money.

He said, "I felt like Furman Bisher [Atlanta sports columnist] on my way to spring training."

Jim never reminded me of Daddy in a physical

sense. He has neither the size nor the personality nor the commanding presence Daddy had.

But they are alike in another way. Above all else, my father was a patriot. So is Jim Minter. There is that manner of men—not as many now as there once were—who believe unhesitatingly in duty, and their courage to do this is far beyond questioning.

Minter was a soldier, too. He was too young for World War II, and he missed out on Korea when he was in the army. But in so many conversations with him over the years, I always noticed a longing in his voice when he talked of war and of serving.

He once said, "You always wonder what you would have done in combat. I wanted to lead in combat, but I never got the chance. What you wonder is whether or not you could have handled it, whether or not you would have screwed up and got yourself killed, or, worse, somebody else."

I have had the same doubts about myself, but not about Minter.

When Daddy died, Jim was the first person I called. He asked me if I needed anything. I said I needed $800 to pay Daddy's hospital bill before they would let me take his body away. Jim put it in my checking account.

A year after I joined the *Journal,* Minter gave me the hardest job I have ever had. I became "slot man," which is the term for the person who gets to work at five each morning and if there is anything wrong with the afternoon sports section that day, it's his fault.

My first wife and I divorced a year after Minter

gave me that job. He said to me later he was afraid that putting me in the slot had surrounded me with pressures that somehow had affected my marriage.

Not so. What affected my first marriage more than anything else was my discovery of the delights of neon. But he cared enough to try to take some of the blame away from me.

Jim Minter has taught me most of what he knows about the sort of values a man should have. I don't have them all, to be sure, but at least I can identify them. All those values are not universally approved of these days. The world has changed a bit on Jim. But for the most part, he hasn't changed with it. That is another reason for my affection for him.

Jim Minter taught me how to write a newspaper column.

"Write short," he said. "Too many columnists write too damn long.

"Don't write cuss words in the newspaper.

"If you think you have a funny line, then don't try to explain it in the next sentence. If it is funny enough, it won't need explaining.

"Don't lose a good source over one quote.

"Every column ought to have at least one human being's name in it and at least one set of quotation marks.

"Don't be out of the newspaper for long stretches of time. People will forget about you.

"Don't forget where you came from."

Jim Minter never has. He was invited, along with a group of other Southern sporting journalists, to the Jimmy Carter White House for a dinner honoring Southern stock-car drivers. Carter had this thing for stock-car racing.

Carter was not able to make the dinner himself, though. He had matters to take up with Begin and Sadat at Camp David.

But it was still an incredible evening. The moon shone brightly behind the Washington Monument as Willie Nelson entertained us on the South Lawn.

Willie was doing "Precious Memories." Minter whispered to me, "My great grandfather was wounded at the Battle of Gettysburg. He had to walk all the way home to Fayette County, Georgia, on one leg. If he was here tonight, he'd think we by-God won."

Jim will not be pleased with what I have written of him in this book. He is not a man who enjoys public scrutiny of any sort.

But I needed to say it. He has punched my ticket for nearly twenty years. I told him once, when I was drunk, that I was afraid of him.

And I am.

I am afraid I will not please him.

If I do it and Jim says it was good, then it was. If he says it was bad, then also so it was. Perhaps it is not wise for a person to put himself in the position of enabling someone else to have that sort of power over him.

But I won't ever stop. In the first place, Jim Minter's standards are to be cherished, rather than avoided. In the second, my daddy was never around to add very much guidance or editorial comment to my efforts and actions. Jim Minter has served in that role for me.

I have been fortunate, as I look back, to have been influenced by the sort of men who have influenced me. I didn't have a daddy around very much when I was a child, and I lost him altogether barely into my adulthood.

But there was Mr. Red and Bob Entrekin and Charlie Bohannon and Pete Moore and George Thompson and my three ex-fathers-in-law, all of whom I never see anymore, to my chagrin, and there has been Jim Minter.

I should have thanked them—and others not named here—for helping to fill out some of the blank spaces left by my daddy. I should have thanked them, but I never have.

This, then, is that overdue thanks.

CHAPTER
12

I WAS A STEPFATHER ONCE FOR THREE YEARS. THERE WERE two children, a boy and a girl. When I married his mother, the little boy was four. His blond hair was constantly falling down over his face. His energy was boundless. He had a passion for toy trucks and playing with them in the dirt.

He was afraid of sleeping without a light.

"He's got to learn to sleep in the dark," I said to his mother. "What happens when he goes to camp or something like that?"

I took it upon myself to teach the little boy to sleep in the dark.

I put him to bed one night. Then, I turned off the light.

He screamed.

"There is nothing in the dark that can hurt you," I said.

That didn't convince him. He continued to

scream. I walked out of his room and shut the door. He got up out of bed and turned the light back on.

I refused to be beaten by a four-year-old. I turned the light back off and told him if he got up and turned it on again I was going to punish him.

He got back up and turned the light on again.

I went in to punish him. I could see the fear in his eyes. I also could see he would take whatever punishment was necessary. He was not going to sleep in the dark.

"You win," I said. I hugged him and kissed him and when I walked out of his room the third time, I left the light on.

The initial most difficult thing I had to accept about my mother marrying my stepfather was that he took my place in her bed. They made a bed out of the sofa in the living room for me. Mama Willie and Daddy Bun had the other bedroom.

Each night I spent alone out there was haunted. It didn't matter there were people in whispering distance from me. Things moved about the room. Dark, scary things, things with no heads and things with more than one head.

I was hurt, angered, and frightened. I turned the lights on in the living room. I banged on the bedroom door and told of awful demons cavorting about. I determined if I was not going to be able to sleep then neither would my mother and stepfather, who had done this horrid thing to me.

My stepfather, H.B., took it upon himself to teach me to sleep alone and with the light off at night.

"Not one more word," he said after I had

knocked on the bedroom door and reported the sighting of a UFO in the kitchen.

I was not going to be outdone by a stepfather.

I banged on the door again five minutes later and said there was something making a noise in the hall closet.

H.B. said there wasn't.

I said there was.

He looked in the closet. The hanging rod had fallen. That's what I had heard.

"The hanging rod fell, that's all it was," H.B. said.

He went back to bed and shut the door.

I turned on the light again.

"Turn that light off," H.B. said from the bedroom.

This was it, I figured.

He came out and looked at me. Maybe what he saw was what I saw in my stepson's face.

"If I let you keep the light on, will you hush and go to sleep?"

Kids deserve to win one occasionally.

Most stepparents never have a chance. They often have all the responsibility of their stepchildren, but they cannot cut through that bond, however mystical it may be, that connects a child to a parent and naturally brings out resentment for anyone else who attempts to step in and establish such a connection.

Being a stepfather myself was an enormous help in finally understanding what H.B. must have gone through with one so dedicated to keeping him from having any control over my life as I most certainly was.

We clashed over most everything. I grew greasy ducktails soon after Elvis made his debut. He demanded I get my hair cut. I demanded that it stay the way it was. When the other kids began referring to me as "Slick," I acquiesced.

One New Year's Eve, there was ice and snow on the roads. An older friend, so the plan went, was picking me up and we were going to a party in Newnan. H.B. said it wasn't safe for me to be out. I argued. He never gave in. I sulked until the third week of February.

What saved us from total war was the little house out back of where we lived. H.B. had worked for a shell home dealer who went bankrupt. What he got instead of a final paycheck was a company Chevrolet and a mini-shell house that had been used at one of the developments for an office. H.B. had the little house moved into our backyard.

When I was fifteen, I moved into it. I had a desk on which to study. I had a phone and a bed and all the comforts, except running water. I still showered in the house and took my meals there. Otherwise, I stayed in the little house, and there were decidedly fewer opportunities for H.B. and me to fall at odds with that living situation.

Betty decided even after the Birmingham fiasco to give it another shot with Daddy. They moved back to East Point outside Atlanta. Daddy somehow convinced a local high school to give him the aforementioned job of teaching Georgia history and mechanical drawing.

After I entered high school, I didn't visit Daddy nearly as often as I had when I was younger. There is a certain independence that comes with the high school years. I had a girl friend, my mother's car most times I asked for it, and I had ball games. The need for Daddy had diminished somewhat, as it does for most who enter the teen years and change from a parent-dominated life to a life influenced mostly by peers.

I graduated high school in June 1964. Each student received two seats for the graduation ceremony. Daddy appeared totally unannounced in Moreland at our house the afternoon before graduation night.

He hadn't been in Moreland since a few days after his return from Korea. I was shocked to see him. Mother was totally flustered. It had been years since they had seen each other.

He was as charming as ever. He was dressed immaculately with the bow tie. Always, the bow tie.

"I've come for my son's graduation," he said to Mother.

"How did you know it was tonight?" I asked him.

"A man should know what night his son is graduating from high school," he answered.

The immediate problem was obvious to me, if not to my mother. There were only the two seats. One for my mother. The other for H.B.

I was astounded at what I was thinking. I was thinking that Daddy hadn't bothered to show up for anything else in my life, and now here he was at my graduation, and he seemed to feel he could just tag along with the three of us.

Suddenly, for the first time in my life, I understood the position H.B. had been in ever since he married my mother. He always came in second to me in almost every situation that called for Mother's attention or affection. He obviously had been completely out of the running in any and every situation that involved Daddy and me. But he had endured it all, and a lesser man might not have.

And here on this night of all nights he would be sent to the back of the bus again. I could picture Daddy at the graduation, taking all the glory for his *mahvelous* son.

I feared there would be a fight. Daddy and H.B. had never met each other. What if it angered H.B. that Daddy was coming to our house? What if he insisted Daddy not go to the graduation?

Mother spoke first. She said, "Lewis, I don't know if it was a good idea for you to come here."

He looked surprised at that statement.

Then she went for the jugular.

"You've disappointed this child so many times. You've not been there when he needed you, or expected you. But tonight, you're here. I don't know if you deserve to see him graduate or not."

It stung him.

"I didn't want to be any trouble," he said. "I just wanted to see my son graduate high school."

Mother had a point, and so did he. But that didn't solve the problem of how H.B. would see all this.

"Do you want me to leave, Christine?" Daddy asked.

I was afraid she would say yes. I was also afraid she would say no. I wanted him there. I couldn't deny that. But I didn't want trouble. I didn't want feelings hurt. I could go and graduate high school alone if it came to that.

Mother hesitated before answering him. She couldn't bring herself to tell him to leave.

"H.B. will be home in a few minutes," she said. "We'll see what he says."

The three of us sat in the living room. The situation was completely awkward. Daddy tried to tell jokes. Mother and I laughed nervously. It would really be a lot simpler, I began thinking, if he would just bow out of this gracefully and there would be no confrontation with H.B.

He didn't, though. I had painted H.B. as a terrible ogre to him. I guess he wanted, if nothing else, to meet the man.

I felt guilty for what all I had said about H.B. and for the way I had treated him. There was the time he gave me the money to go to the Gator Bowl in Jacksonville with some of my friends when Mother had insisted he not do it.

There was the day I turned sixteen and went to get my driver's license. I had been marking off the days for a year. He drove me thirty miles to LaGrange to take the driver's test, and I had to show my learner's permit before I could take it. I hadn't known that. I didn't have my learner's permit with me.

It was Saturday. I had a date that night, my first

where I drove the car. I was devastated by the news that I couldn't get my license.

H.B. drove me back to Moreland, then drove me *back* to LaGrange with my learner's permit. I got my license. He let me drive home. I kept my date. My life would have been temporarily ruined if I hadn't.

And he'd finally gotten off my back about the chores. He let me drink a beer with him occasionally. And eating the English peas at the father-son dinner hadn't been that awful of an experience, now that I thought about it.

H.B. drove into the driveway. I prepared for the worst. I am certain Mother did, too.

Daddy rose from his chair and walked toward H.B. as he opened the front door.

"I'm Lewis Grizzard," he said to H.B.

H.B. was startled for a moment. But he regained his composure and the two men shook hands. Mine were trembling.

"He's here for the graduation," Mother said, almost defensively.

"Well, good," H.B. said.

I couldn't believe he said that.

"I hope I'm not interfering," Daddy said. This was too good to be true.

But there remained the problem of the seats. I had only two. I finally spoke up.

"Daddy, we've only got two seats in the auditorium."

"I'll just stand in the back," he said. I hadn't thought of that. I felt a little better.

"No," said H.B. "I'll be glad to stand up. You and Christine are his parents."

For the first time, I saw my daddy rendered speechless. He finally spat out, "That's very kind, but you don't have to do . . ."

H.B. said, "I insist."

The three of them, my mother, my daddy, and my stepfather, drove to the graduation together in H.B.'s car. I drove my mother's. There was a party for the graduates at the Elks Club in Newnan after the ceremonies.

Daddy and Mother sat together while they passed out the diplomas. H.B. stood in the back.

I changed a great deal that night. I think more than anything else, I realized beyond any doubt that I had been fortunate to have a mother who stood by me and a stepfather who made her life better and who had put some stability—no matter how much I had rejected it—into mine.

I found Daddy with the principal of the high school when I came off the stage.

"You've done such a *mahvelous* job with our son," he was saying. "His mother and I appreciate it so much."

H.B. stood behind him with Mother and said nothing.

I went to my party. Mother said Daddy stayed in Moreland for about an hour and that he had been very grateful to H.B. for giving him his seat.

The graduation party was wonderful. My girl friend gave me certain unexpected post-graduation liberties. Ronnie Jenkins and I iced down a case of beer in the back of the car, and we slipped out away from the dancing every now and then to have one.

I got home at eight the next morning, slept a few

hours, and then left home for a summer job in Atlanta.

Driving away from Moreland, I sensed there never would be a night quite as fulfilling as the one that had just passed. For a few hours, I had it all.

Betty sent Daddy packing for the last time soon after I graduated. Bob witnessed the last straw.

"Mother called me and said Lewis had disappeared the day before and still wasn't home. No matter what he did, she still worried about him.

"Of course, I knew what had happened. He was off on another bender. It was like clockwork. For a while, he's fine. Then off he would go, chasing that bottle.

"I left work and went to hunt for him. I normally checked all the motels and any sort of VFW or American Legion post around. He could sit down at a bar at one of those places and spin a few battle yarns and he would own the place.

"Sure enough, I found him at a VFW. He said, 'Roh-but, what a pleasant surprise,' when I walked in. It was a surprise, all right, but I'm certain it wasn't pleasant.

"He was pretty well oiled by that time, but at least he was still among the living. He left with me quietly. When I got him home, Nanny told him to go down to the second-floor bedroom and take a shower and get a little nap and she would fix him something to eat. He agreed.

"We sat in the kitchen and talked about what to do with him for about a half hour while she cooked. I know it hadn't been longer than that. When she finished, she called out to him to come to eat. There was no response. She called again.

"Finally, I went down to check on him, and he was gone. There was no trace of his ever being there. I couldn't believe he could get away again that fast.

"I looked all over East Point for him, and I came up completely empty. He didn't have any extra clothes with him, he didn't have his shaving kit, and I doubt he had much money. But he was gone."

He turned up next, several months later, in Athens, where I had just begun my freshman year at the university. I'm not certain how he located me. The man moved in mysterious, yet often effective, ways. He called my dorm and left a message to call him back.

"Where are you?" I asked him.

"I've got the most mahvelous job, right here in Athens," he said. "I'm the manager of the Davis Brothers Cafeteria."

Amazing.

I told him my room number. He said he would be right over. A cab dropped him off. I introduced him to my roommate. They exchanged greetings that lasted about ten seconds. That becomes important later.

"I wanted to be as close to you as I could, son," he said.

I could sense even then our relationship was changing. I had needed him for so long. And now, he needed me. There was no more Betty to take care of him. Uncle Frank and Aunt Jessie, his brother and sister, had died. His well-being was now being passed along to me.

I had a part-time job at the local newspaper. I had a full load of courses, and I was interested in the social aspects of college life, as well. He became a bit of a pain.

I could feel him clinging to me now.

"This is a new beginning for me, son," he said.

I also could feel the pressure and the guilt. I loved him. I cared for him, but he was interfering in the new beginning I had.

On the weekends, I usually drove to Atlanta to see my girl friend. He seemed at times to resent that. "The weekend is the only time I have to see you," he said. Guilt.

He insisted I eat at his cafeteria as often as I could.

"Daddy, I can't eat with you tonight," I would begin.

"In the name of God, why not, son?"

"I'm going out with my friends."

"You didn't come eat last night."

"I had to study."

"And you're probably going away for the week-end, too." More guilt.

We had some good times, though. My job with the paper was covering local high school sports. We made a few basketball games together. He would sit behind me at the scorer's desk and shout instructions to both teams. Others at the scorer's table would turn around to see who this man was.

"Hello," he said to somebody one night, "I'm

Major Grizzard. My son is covering this game for the paper."

I joined a fraternity. Daddy immediately dropped by the house one night to meet everybody. He just happened to bring a large supply of fried chicken and pies from the cafeteria for my brothers. They took to him immediately. He told a joke or two, related a few war stories, and they were his. More on that later, too.

He met some people called the Peaveys.

"Mahvelous people, the Peaveys," he said to me at supper one night. "They are a gospel singing group, and they want me to join them in a performance Sunday afternoon. Please come along."

We took a cab Sunday afternoon to the outskirts of Athens to a small framed country church. One of the marquees-on-wheels was out front of the church. It said, GOSPEL SINGING, 3:00 P.M.

The Peaveys were Mr. Peavey and Mrs. Peavey and three of the little Peaveys. Mrs. Peavey played piano while the others sang. They were terrible, and it was hot inside that little church. People cleared their throats and fanned themselves with those old-fashioned church fans, the ones the politicians used to provide.

Mr. Peavey introduced Daddy. "Major Lewis Grizzard, my dear friend, is going to join us for one of my favorite hymns—praise the Lord—'Just as I Am.'"

Daddy, to quote a phrase used most often, *turned the place out*. He sat down at the piano and took command of "Just as I Am." His voice eventually silenced the Peaveys. Then, he did, "Just a Closer

Walk with Thee," "What a Friend We Have in Jesus," and for a finale, he did "Tennessee Waltz." Nobody noticed, I don't think, "Tennessee Waltz" is not a hymn.

"Major Grizzard," some little lady said after the performance, "I have never heard such sangin' in my life. You are a blessing."

The rest of the congregation thanked him as well. The minister said, "You're welcome anytime at our church, Major Grizzard." He was back the next Sunday to lead the congregation's *sangin'* and two weeks later, the minister asked if he would like to stand in for him and bring the day's message.

I was there. It was a thing of beauty. He talked of being in that hole in Korea and Jesus coming to him in a vision and telling him not to fear.

He quoted scripture I am certain never really existed. He would speak softly and then slowly bring it to a crescendo that would have chased the devil out of that church and three surrounding counties.

After the service, we were invited to one of the deacon's homes for lunch. We ate like kings. Later, Daddy sat down at the deacon's piano and rendered another resounding performance.

The deacon drove us back to the boardinghouse where Daddy was living. Daddy hit him for a twenty. The man seemed overwhelmed to do him, as he said, "such a small favor."

I'm not certain how much Daddy finally took away from members of the church, not to mention the Peaveys and three cooks at the cafeteria, several of my fraternity brothers, several of his fellow boarders at a local rooming house where he lived, but suddenly, he had a pocketful of cash and the inevitable occurred.

He caught a ride out of town, and I didn't hear from him again for nearly six months. His whereabouts during that time remain a mystery, but after spring vacation, my roommate came back and said my father had called his house in a small south Georgia town and had asked him for twenty dollars. He met my roommate once. He was with him for ten seconds. Yet, six months later, he remembered his name, his hometown, and found a way to reach him. The man was a genius. And incidentally, my roommate had given him the twenty. I was the one who paid him back.

It was utterly amazing how he could get money off people. Bob tells of the time he received a telephone call from a perfect stranger when he was still in Birmingham, some months after Daddy had gone east.

"Do you know a Major Lewis Grizzard?" the man asked.

"I do, indeed," said Bob.

"Well, he owes me five hundred dollars. Do you know where he is?"

"I haven't the slightest."

"I cosigned a note with him at the bank. He's not going to get away with this."

"Oh, yes he is, too," said Bob.

"What do you mean?"

"Let me ask you something. How long did you know Major Grizzard before you cosigned the note with him?"

"A couple of hours."

"My friend," Bob said, "you have just joined one of the largest fraternities in the South. What you should do is forget about the five hundred and save yourself a great deal of grief."

Ronnie Jenkins, my friend from high school, had met my daddy. He was quite impressed with the Major. I said to Ronnie, "One day, I don't know when, the Major is going to contact you and want a favor. He may want you to come and get him and give him a ride. He probably will also ask you to lend him some money. If you could give him some assistance in getting from one place to another, I would appreciate it. But leave your money at home."

"He couldn't talk me out of any money," Ronnie said.

"Yes, he could," I assured him.

Some months after that, Daddy was stuck in Hogansville, a small town south of Grantville, where Ronnie lived. He called Ronnie and asked if he would give him a ride to Atlanta. Ronnie agreed.

"You remembered to leave your money at home, I hope," I said to Ronnie when he told me of the incident later.

"I left it at home, just like you told me," Ronnie said. "But the Major was in such a bad way, I went back home and got it and let him have a ten."

My daddy had some measure of pride left, I am certain, but he never allowed it to stand in the way of a handout when he so desperately needed one. He soon discovered mission homes for alcoholic men.

They were a godsend for him. They usually were run by ministers, who were always an easy touch for Daddy. They offered warm meals and a place to spend a little time with no payment expected.

His favorite was Hope Haven, near Jefferson, Georgia, in the northeast section of the state. I wrote a newspaper column about Hope Haven, and my father's connections to it, some years ago. A woman who worked there remembered "the Major" fondly.

"He'd come to us in an awful shape," she said. "We'd take him in and he'd sleep it off. Then, he'd take a shower, and we'd give him a clean, white shirt, and he'd come out with that bow tie on, looking like a million dollars.

"The other men loved him because he was always carrying on with them about something. You know what a good personality he had.

"He'd sit down at the piano and play just about anything you wanted him to play. He'd always play 'When the Saints Go Marching In' for me.

"The other men looked up to him and respected him because he'd been in the war and all. I think he helped a lot of those men. I just wish somebody could have helped him."

He was in another home for a couple of weeks in South Carolina. He wrote me in Athens to tell me how *mahvelous* the place was and how much the minister there was helping him.

I found the number of the home, called it, and asked for Lewis Grizzard.

"The Major?" the voice on the other end asked. "He left a couple of days ago."

"Did he say where he was going?"

"He said he was going to see his son, but he'd be back in a week or so. We took up some money and bought him bus fare."

"Do you happen to have a piano there?" I asked.

"Yes we do."

"And did Mr. Grizzard play for you?"

"Played and sang all the time."

The Major strikes again.

He came back to Athens one more time, spring quarter of my sophomore year. I had an efficiency apartment. I was planning to marry in the summer. Daddy had another job in no time. He took over the food service for the Georgian Hotel. All he ever needed was five minutes of an employer's time and the job was his. I would meet him for lunch at a campus sandwich shop.

"Just what I need," he said, "a little sandwich shop right here on the campus."

Luckily, the sandwich shop had no piano, or it would have been his.

After a month or so, he tired of the room they had given him at the hotel, and he asked if he could move in with me.

"Only until you get married," he said.

I didn't see any harm in it. He moved his few belongings in. I worked nights and went to class days. We still didn't see that much of each other, except for our lunches.

But it was a nice time. We were living under the same roof for the first time since I was six. There was only one problem. I began smoking after high school. Daddy hated smoking. I can remember as a child his saying to me, "I don't want ever to see one of those ol' cigarettes hanging out of your mouth. Let old guhls [girls] smoke those things."

I stopped smoking in the apartment. Despite what he had put me through with all the disappearances and all the disappointments, I still couldn't bring myself to smoke a cigarette in front of him. The desire for parental support and the fear of parental rebuke has no age limit in most of us.

It was a Friday in May 1966 when my future mother-in-law called me in Athens to say my intended had been hospitalized, in Atlanta, suffering from abdominal pains.

"Should I come?" I asked.

"She's scared. I think she would like to see you."

There was some high drama to this. Fiancée calls for lover at her hospital bedside. I called Daddy at work and told him I was leaving for Atlanta.

"I'll go with you, son," he said.

He sounded supportive of my problem. I welcomed that.

We drove out of Athens in my blue VW. I began to crave a cigarette. The craving got worse.

I didn't know if I could do it. I didn't know if I could pull out a cigarette and smoke it in front of my daddy. How would he react? Would he think me a weakling for falling into the clutches of the weed he so abhorred?

What am I saying? I thought to myself. He is an alcoholic. When it came to booze and me, he always chose booze, didn't he? What right did he have to look down on me for smoking?

I did recall Daddy comparing drinking and smoking once, however. He said, "At least when you drink, you get drunk. You don't get anything out of an ol' cigarette but yellow teeth and bad breath."

I reached for the cigarettes in my coat pocket several times. Each time that I did, however, I returned my hand to the steering wheel.

This was silly. Here I am on the way to see my wife-to-be who has been hospitalized, I'm nervous enough as it is, and I'm afraid to light up a cigarette in front of my father.

I pulled off just before the interstate to Atlanta. I needed gasoline. I also needed a cigarette. I looked the man in the face and said, "Daddy, I smoke."

It may have been the three most difficult words I'd ever forced out of my mouth. I was filled with both shame and anticipation.

"You do what?" he asked me. There wasn't that much of a hint of disdain in his voice. It was more like he didn't understand what I had said.

"I smoke, Daddy," I repeated myself. "And I'm very nervous about all this right now, and if you don't mind, I need a cigarette."

"Go ahead," he said. "If you're old enough to get married, I guess you're old enough to start smoking."

I pulled the pack of Marlboros from inside my coat pocket, pushed in the lighter in the car, and waited an eternity until it popped out. I took the lighter in hand, lit the cigarette, put the lighter back, and took a deep drag of the smoke. I blew it out the window.

"I didn't smoke when I played ball, Daddy," I said. "I want you to know that."

I was grasping for straws now. It was incredible how I felt. I felt ashamed. I felt weak in front of my daddy. I tried emergency rationalizing.

Why should I be doing this to myself? The woman I loved was in the hospital, and here I was more concerned about whether or not a daddy who had let me down so much felt as if I had somehow betrayed him.

"In the name of God, son," he finally said to me, "if you want to smoke, it's fine. I'm not that proud of everything I do, either."

"You don't hate me, do you, Daddy?" I asked him.

"I don't hate you."

"Promise?"

"You're my son. I love you."

We sat staring at each other, both a bit uncomfortable. For the first time as an adult, I was interacting with my father on a level beyond merely being courteous with one another.

I was seeking his blessing, and his forgiveness, too, for that matter. And he had given me both.

"I love you, Daddy," I said to him. I couldn't remember how long it had been since I had said that to him.

"In the name of God, son," he replied, "we need to get on to the hospital."

I flipped my cigarette out the window and drove away. I felt the elation of having just made a new friend.

The hospital scare turned out to be nothing more than a case of gastritis. I dropped Daddy off downtown before I went to the hospital. He needed to see a man, he said.

Maybe an hour after I dropped him, he walked into the hospital room carrying some packages. He had met my wife-to-be only once before, very briefly, the night of our high school graduation. It rarely mattered to Daddy how long he had known someone, or how well. He would give to them, or take from them, based only upon his need, or theirs, at the particular time.

He had brought a dress and a blouse for the patient. He even had the sizes right. She appeared to be pleased with the styles, as well.

"You really have great taste in women's clothes, Mr. Grizzard," she said.

"Call me Major, my dear," he replied.

I never knew how much of Daddy's charm was actually premeditated groundwork for the future. Maybe he thought if he bore her gifts, then down the line somewhere, on a cold, lonely, and sober night, she could be of help to him. It was a rotten thought, but I'd seen his pattern too many times not to be a bit suspicious.

"I really like Mr. Grizzard," she said to me as I left the hospital.

"Call him the Major," I heard myself saying to her.

I was concerned that when we married in July, and he would have to leave the apartment, he would be off again on another bender. I could sense in him a loneliness I had never really seen, perhaps because I hadn't noticed or perhaps because he had not shown it before. He had never clung to me. Until then.

I didn't have to wait for the wedding. I came home from work one night and found him asleep on his bed, with an empty bottle of Ezra Brooks bourbon on the table beside him. He was sitting on the side of his bed when I awakened the next morning, in obvious distress.

"You don't know where I could get a little drink, do you, son?" he asked.

His eyes were swollen and red.

"Where did you get what you had last night?" I asked him.

"From a cab driver," he answered.

Athens was officially dry, with the exception of beer and wine.

"I can get you some beer," I said.

"Ol' beer won't do very much good."

"How about some wine?"

"What I need is a good drink of whiskey."

People in hell need ice water, too, I thought to myself.

A fraternity brother lived a few apartments down. I said I would go and see if he had any booze.

This particular individual had immaculate taste for a nineteen-year-old, as well as a stipend from home to keep it satisfied. He drove a Corvette, had a closetful of Gant shirts, and he figured to have a good whiskey stash.

"I haven't made a run to South Carolina to restock my bar," he told me when I delivered my request. "All I've got left is a little Wild Turkey."

"Daddy needs a drink bad," I said.

"Take it if it will do him any good."

I knew about Wild Turkey. It was one of the most expensive bourbons you could buy. I felt I had made the ultimate score.

"You're in luck," I said to Daddy. "He had a little Wild Turkey left. This is about as good a bourbon as you can buy."

"Let me have it, please," he said.

He filled up a glass and placed the empty bottle next to the other one beside his bed. He turned the glass up and did not put it down until all the Wild Turkey was gone.

"Mahvelous," he critiqued the drink.

I showered and shaved and got ready for class. When I walked back into the bedroom, he was lying down.

"I hope you're going to get up and go to work," I said.

"I'm much too ill," he said.

"Too hung over, you mean."

"Sick, sick, sick. In the name of God, I am sick."

"They'll fire you."

"You can't fire a man who is on the brink of death."

I frowned.

"Don't hate me," Daddy said.

"I don't hate you. I just wish you'd get up and go to work."

"I'll try, if you will do me one more little favor."

"What's that?"

"I need another little drink."

"You just had a drink of Wild Turkey," I said.

"Indeed," he replied, "but I believe my Wild Turkey has flown away."

I left him there. When I came home that evening, he was gone. I didn't see him again for over a year.

My girlfriend and I married in Moreland, July 17, 1966. We drove away in my blue VW, bound for Myrtle Beach, South Carolina, for our honeymoon. We made it as far as Greenville, South Carolina, where we spent our wedding night.

The next morning, as we drove on toward the beach, I thought about what I had just done and why I had done it.

I loved her. There was no doubt about that. I had loved her for six years. I rarely had dated anyone else in that time. She remained my lone experience with a lover.

I hadn't been living the life of the footloose collegian before we married, either. Days, I went to school. I worked nights. I drove to Atlanta to see her on weekends. It made sense to me to have her in Athens on a full-time basis.

There was something else, too, and I first realized it the morning we drove toward Myrtle Beach. What I was doing here was re-creating what I had missed so much as a child.

I was my daddy. She was his wife. We were Lewis and Christine, Part Two. I had wanted my mother and father to be together for so long, and that never was to be.

But I could have this. I could salvage what I had lost this way. I caught myself playing Daddy to her

Mother. I called my wife the pet names my father had called my mother. "Pearl" was his favorite.

It all felt fine. The third or fourth night of our honeymoon, we went to a restaurant that had dancing and a band.

We danced to Sinatra's "Summer Wind" and Marvin Gaye's "Stubborn Kind of Fellow." When the band asked for requests, I had one.

I wrote "Tennessee Waltz" on the napkin and handed it to the band leader.

CHAPTER
13

I PARKED MY CAR, THE BLUE VW, IN THE OLD UNION STA-tion parking lot, which was next door to the *Journal-Constitution* building at 10 Forsyth Street in Atlanta. It was January 1968.

It was my first day with the *Journal*. I had bought a new sports coat at an outlet store. I had my hair slicked down. The "dry look" had not emerged at that time.

I caught the elevator to the fourth floor and tried not to look nervous. I walked into the *Journal* sports department, a small office tucked away from the rest of the newsroom. There were five or six men seated around a horseshoe desk.

I asked for "Mr. Minter."

Nobody looked up. Finally, the "slot man" said, "He doesn't come in until eight-thirty or nine."

It was seven in the morning. I took a seat near the

desk where Minter had initially interviewed me for the job.

Fifteen minutes later, the assistant sports editor, Tom McCollister, said, "Have you come here to work?"

"Mr. Minter hired me," I said.

"Well, then get your butt over here and go to work," McCollister said.

I filled an empty seat around the desk. The slot man tossed me a wire story on which to write a headline. It was a "1–0," two lines of 24-point, all caps. There was room for only two short words on each line.

The story was about Davey Bristol, the Cincinnati Reds' manager, who had become ill.

I didn't want to screw this up. I didn't want to fail my first assignment. This was the *Atlanta* by-God *Journal,* the big time. Many of those around me had been at the paper when I was a kid. I had just joined the Yankees and here I was taking batting practice with Mantle, Maris, and Berra.

BRISTOL ILL, for the first line, but I couldn't think of anything for the second. I began to perspire. I wondered to myself why nobody on the desk talked to each other, much less to me.

I tried the headline again. I was writing it out with a pencil on a sheet of brown copy paper:

DAVE BRISTOL
TAKEN ILL

That was my second attempt, but the second line did not fill out. I could feel myself reaching the panic stage. I had to hit one out of the park here so the veterans wouldn't think there was a masquerader in their midst.

I wrote:

REDS' BRISTOL
HOSPITALIZED

Perfect. I tossed the wire story and the headline back to McCollister. He grunted approval, and called for a copyboy (you can no longer call newsroom gofers "copyboys"; they now are "carrier persons") to send them down the pneumatic tubes to the composing room.

Maybe I hadn't homered my first day with the big club, but I felt I had at least hit a few line drives. Still, nobody talked to me. I went back to the chair near Minter's desk and sat down. One of the writers I didn't know, a man named Frank Hyland, walked over and introduced himself.

"I've been here only two weeks myself," he said, "and that's about how long it takes for anybody to start speaking to you."

"The silent treatment finally stops, huh?" I replied.

"Once they get to know you," Frank said.

They were an odd assortment, my new colleagues. McCollister was a short, feisty man, who got that way, I was to learn later, from all those mornings of getting to work at 5 A.M.

Wilt Browning was the baseball writer. He actually spoke to me before the ice finally melted. That was because he rarely came into the office and wasn't certain if I had been on the staff for months.

Teague Jackson was the golf writer. He was a big man with thick glasses whose father had been financial editor of the *Chicago Tribune.* He was from Michigan. I'd never worked with anybody from up north before.

Darrell Simmons, who reminded me of Hoss Cartwright, covered pro football. Bill Clark was college editor. He had all this hair and when he typed, he would stop every few words to run his hands through his hair.

Hyland covered pro basketball and soccer. He was from Minnesota but he'd just been hired from West Palm Beach, Florida. There was something about Frank I liked a great deal.

Bill Whitley, as round as he was tall, covered high-school sports. He was a Georgia man, too. There was Minter, the executive sports editor, of course, and then two other people, both of whom were legends to me.

One was Furman Bisher, the sports editor, the brilliant columnist, the host of "Football Review." I'd read everything he had written since I was ten.

He was, and is, a magician with words. One of my favorite columns of his concerned riding with the now-departed Crackers, the city's minor league team, on a train trip to Little Rock. That's when I decided I wanted to ride trains and write things about such exotic places as Little Rock.

Bisher, my colleagues told me, was a man to be wary of. They told of how Bisher once had run the office as well as write his column, and that, after a near mutiny by the staff, the duties of taking care of the daily paper had been passed along to Minter.

Bisher's office was a sort of small cage inside the office. He came in even later than Minter. He was, and is, a handsome man, with a certain charm that belies any tendencies to hardheadedness and a hair-trigger temper.

But there were all those stories about him.

"I don't care what anybody tells you," the stories usually began, "Bisher rules this place. We had another guy here who said, 'When Bisher calls you into his office, you're in trouble. In there, he is undefeated, untied and unscored upon.'"

They told the one about the time Bisher fired a guy.

"This guy was a terrible writer, but he was very gung ho. Bisher didn't like him very much.

"One morning, Bisher walks in and says to this guy across the office, 'I've got a great new assignment for you.'

"So the guy jumps up and says, 'Really, Bish? What is it?'

"Bisher said, 'Find yourself another job.'"

I heard all the stories of the temper tantrums and how if Bisher was shot, it would take six months to round up everybody with a motive.

He often conferred with Minter in his office. I lived in constant fear of Bisher. I always was afraid when Minter went into his office, they were talking about me and Bisher was saying, "You've got to get rid of this guy Grizzard."

Bill Robinson, the veteran racing and outdoor writer, came into the office even later than both

Minter and Bisher. In fact, it was three weeks after I went to work that Robinson came in at all.

The first time I saw him in person, he strode in with a bundle of books and papers and took a seat at his desk. The rest of us wore ties. Minter insisted. Robinson had on a pair of jeans, a shirt that looked like a pajama top, and a Pure Oil cap.

Robinson's desk was next to mine. As soon as he put down his papers and books, he turned around to me and said, "I'm Bill Robinson. Are you the new guy, 'Grizzard'?"

"It's Griz-ZARD," I said.

"It came close to being 'Gizzard,' though," he said with a smile.

There was a charm to Robinson, too. It was different from Bisher's, but it was there. He had a sort of drowsy look about him. And his right eye tended to droop a little. He had a warm, deep voice, and he smiled out of one side of his mouth.

For some reason, Robinson took me under his wing. He called me "Young Gene Talmadge." Gene Talmadge had been a firebrand governor of the state. His son, Herman, was in the Senate.

Robinson was a bit of a historian.

"When Gene used to ride in his Model-T back to Atlanta after a weekend at home down in McRae, he'd stop in every little town on the way and the farmers would load him up with everything he wanted. He'd get back to the capital with live chickens and eggs and ham and homemade bread with jams and preserves. He might not have been Georgia's best governor, but he was the best fed.

"He'd go out to stump the state and he'd make a

speech in front of the county courthouse. He would always plant a few of his people around, some of them in trees, and they would throw planted questions at him.

"One would always say, 'Tell 'em 'bout them lyin' Atlanta newspapers, Gene,' and he'd say, 'I'm a-comin' to that.' I saw a picture of ol' Gene when he was young. You look a lot like him."

I was, by no means, a Gene Talmadge scholar, but I took it as a compliment.

There were Robinson stories, too. Hundreds of them.

"We had a slot man once named Greg Farve," somebody was saying. "He was a Cajun and had a quick temper. Robinson was always late in the mornings, and Farve was always on him about it. One day, when Robinson got off the elevator, he was rolling a tire. He rolled it into the office and said to Farve, 'I knew you wouldn't believe me if I said I had a flat tire, so I brought you the tire.' Later, Robinson admitted he had been carrying that tire in his truck for years, just in case of such an emergency."

Robinson had eight children and a wife. Some months after the tire incident, Farve again tired of his lateness, so another story went, and said to Robinson, "I don't care what your excuse is, Robinson. The next time you're late, you're fired. I promise you."

The next morning Robinson was late. Farve called him over.

"You know what I said, Robinson," he began.

"You're going to fire me, right?" Robinson asked.

"Yes, I'm going to fire you," Farve went on, "but just for the record, what is your excuse?"

"Greg," Robinson began, "you know I've been married nine years."

"What's that got to do with anything?" Farve shot back.

"Well, we've been married nine years, and we have eight children, and this is the first time since we've been married my wife's had her period, and she felt so bad, I had to cook breakfast for the kids and take them to school."

Farve, the story went on, buried his head in his hands on the desk. Robinson had saved himself again.

Robinson, after he had known me for only a couple of weeks, made me assistant outdoor editor. We carried an outdoor page twice a week and each page included such information as lake levels and fishing outlooks. This was obtainable from the state Game and Fish Department.

First, Robinson allowed me to call Game and Fish for him in order to get the lake levels and fishing reports. I was flattered. Later, he discovered I could lay out a page, so he put me in charge of laying out the outdoor pages twice a week. Then he found out I knew my way around the composing room, so he put me in charge of going to the composing room to oversee his pages.

"You do good work," he said.

I thanked him.

Some weeks after my appointment, Minter gave me an assignment to cover a football practice.

"I can't," I said. "I have to lay out the outdoor page."

"Why do you have to do that?" he asked.

"I'm Mr. Robinson's assistant."

"What?"

"Mr. Robinson made me his assistant and I'm laying out the outdoor pages now."

Minter turned red with rage.

"There is no such position as assistant outdoor editor," he said. "Find Robinson and tell him to get his ass in here and do his own job."

Robinson was the best pure writer on the regular staff. His stock car racing reports were things of beauty. One day, he sent the following lead back from Daytona.

DAYTONA BEACH, FLA.—*Richard (the Hemi-Hearted) Petty, piloting his low-slung Blue Angel Plymouth No. 42, flat-out and with its belly to the ground, chased a hurrying sundown here Thursday and caught the final checkers with no one else in sight to win the Daytona Firecracker 400.*

Brilliant. He had another that was unforgettable.

DAYTONA BEACH, FLA.—*Cale Yarborough and Charlie Glotzbach, two ol' five-and-dimers who had been here before, came to the final quarter-mile of the Daytona 500 nose-to-nose, wheel-to-wheel, as the seconds ticked away like drumbeats.*

When the checkers fell a lifetime later, Yarborough had won by a length of what is left of the hairs on his balding head.

Where Robinson was long on talent, he often was somewhat short on accuracy, but that never slowed

him from concocting scenes of which a novelist
would be proud.

Robinson was constantly in trouble with Minter,
and when you got into trouble with Minter, he
would assign you the cruel fate of covering a high-
school sporting event.

Robinson fell on Minter's bad side during the
high-school football playoffs, and he assigned
Robinson to cover a game in extreme north Georgia
on a rainy, foggy Friday night.

We all knew Robinson would not make the game.
There was no way he was going to drive 180 miles
round trip to watch two high-school teams in the
rain and cold. We also knew, however, that somehow Robinson would have a story.

I was in the slot the Saturday morning after the
ball game. Robinson showed late, as usual. I was on
my way to the composing room. I told him the
length to write, and I asked him also to give me a
line score and set of statistics.

"Something happened last night at the *Constitution*
[the morning paper]," I said, "and they have only
one paragraph on the game and no line scores and
statistics."

I could see panic set in on Robinson's face. I
knew why. He had not gone to the game and was
planning to tap-dance his way through by rewriting
the story in the morning papers.

But Robinson was magnificent in the clutch. I got
my story, and it was a thing of beauty. He wrote of
the "chilled dampness that rolled in off the mountains of north Georgia" and the "autumnal brown-

ing of the turf on which the young men of both gallant teams trod."

He had great quotes from both coaches. And, he had a line score and a set of statistics. He made them up, too.

Working in a sports department was a man's world. I had Minter's militaristic rules and values to follow. I had Bisher on a mountain of esteem. I had Robinson for humor. This was my place. I belonged here. This was my combat and these were my comrades. Finally, I had generals and captains and fellow PFCs. I flourished in this. Less than three years after I began work, Minter moved upstairs to become managing editor of the *Constitution,* and I was named executive sports editor in his place. I was twenty-three, and I was a commanding officer.

I was something else, too. I was fat. Here is what happened:

I had been skinny all my life. I am back to skinny now. When I was in high school, they called me "the stick." No matter how small a basketball uniform I wore, I still had those tiny arms and legs sticking out of it. Mothers of friends always wanted to feed me when I visited their homes.

After I married, I quit exercising and took up beer-drinking on a full-time basis. Because an afternoon newspaper staff begins its day in the early hours of morning, we were off soon after the final edition was completed, at one in the afternoon.

After a few months at the *Journal,* I became friends with Frank Hyland, Bill Whitley, and Darrell Simmons.

Frank was a beer drinker's beer drinker. Each afternoon after work, we followed him to one of Atlanta's favorite drinkeries, Manuel's Tavern, where they sold draft beer for a mere quarter a glass. We drank beer each day from shortly after one until shortly before five, when we all were expected home to greet our working wives.

How I got fat is that I would drink all that beer and then my country-reared wife would fill the table with the type of food I like best. The weekly fare went something like this:

Monday—Fried chicken, mashed potatoes with gravy, hot biscuits.

Tuesday—Country fried steak, mashed potatoes with gravy, hot buttered biscuits.

Wednesday—Pork chops, etc.

Thursday—Fried chicken again, etc.

Friday—Spaghetti with gobs of sauce and an assortment of buttered breads.

The Weekends—I pigged out at various fast-fooderies and ate a lot of donuts and other such health foods.

I went from 135 when I graduated from high school to a rotund 210 by the time I was twenty-two.

"You're getting fat," people said to me.

I, frankly, was glad that I was, and it all had to do with my father again. He had blossomed into 240 after his ordeal in Korea. I wanted to be a big man. I was tired of being thin. I resembled my father only slightly when I weighed 135. When I weighed 210 —most of it in my face and stomach—it was remarkable how our resemblance had grown stronger.

It was another opportunity to play him. I not

only had my own command and a good wife, but now I even looked like the man.

I could put it all together here. I could re-create my own version of Daddy's life and make it work out as his had not. The only thing missing in my scheme was a son.

We tried. Nothing happened. We tried again and again, and still nothing happened. We went to see a doctor. He wanted a sperm count from me. It was on the low side of normal.

"You're a newspaper man, aren't you?" the doctor asked me. I nodded yes.

"We often find low sperm counts in men who have certain occupations. One is the newspaper business. I suppose there is a great deal of stress in that profession, and that causes the sperm count to be low."

I asked if this meant we couldn't have any children.

"Certainly not," he said. "We need to run some more tests on your wife."

The problem turned out to be something amiss with her. He mentioned an operation. We said we would get back to him, which we never did.

She was a grand wife. She was pretty and she laughed and she could cook. God, how she could cook.

And we had never known any sort of relationship—I despise that word, but I can't remember what we used to say before we said "relationship"—other than the one we had with each other.

But we were young, and I was changing. My ambition was controlling me. So were the delights I was suddenly finding in places I'd never known before—dimly lit places with music and laughter and girls in short pants and high boots and men who had slipped their wedding rings into their pockets.

The marriage became cumbersome to me. It got in the way of what else was out there. It is difficult to blink at neon, I discovered. I put my wedding band in my pocket one night. After that, it was easy.

Three years after we married, we separated. A few months later, we divorced. She remarried. Later, she had her babies.

We had fought only once over Daddy. He had visited us on occasion, and he had been as charming as ever. He never came to the house without some gift for her.

I don't recall ever explaining how I felt about him to her. She knew mostly only what others in Moreland knew, which was I had a daddy and that he had been in the war, but there had been some sort of disgrace and he didn't live with me and my mother anymore.

Daddy spent his last couple of years near coastal Savannah. He would ride the *Nancy Hanks* passenger train into Atlanta and he spent an occasional weekend with us in the new $23,000 house we bought in suburban Atlanta.

My wife was pleasant to him, and she laughed at his stories, but I could sense that she had some mistrust of him.

I asked her if there were a problem.

"I don't want you giving him any of our money," she said.

Her reply shocked me.

"He's my daddy," I said. "Sometimes I have to help him out a little."

"It's my money, too, and I don't want you giving it to him so he can drink it up."

I had the same reaction I had when my grandmother or any other of my relatives had spoken unkindly of Daddy. I was resentful. I defended him.

"He may drink, but he's been in two wars," I said. "Your daddy didn't fight in a war."

"He never left me and my mother, either," she said.

Why couldn't I convince anybody of this man's greatness? Didn't they ever stop to think of what he did in the army? Didn't they know going through combat and getting wounded and seeing men die could change a man?

"He won the Bronze Star, goddammit," I said to my wife.

Daddy most certainly had become my burden, one that I would have to carry alone. His remaining brothers and sisters had thrown up their arms. Mother wasn't even remotely in his life anymore. Betty and Bob were out of it, too. And my wife had made it clear to me she did not want him interfering in our lives.

A few months later, the burden got heavier. They called me from the little county hospital in Metter, Georgia, near Savannah. Daddy had suffered a stroke.

I drove down to see him. He was having convulsions and didn't know I was there. I had the hospital bring in a rollaway bed so I could sleep beside him.

He had some friends who came to see him, people he had met at his church. Listening to them was familiar.

"We love the Major," they said. "He has brought us so much happiness at our church. He plays and sings so well."

A man named John came to visit.

"I'm a veteran just like your daddy," he said.

John was also a juicer. I knew that by the rasp of his voice and the red of his eyes.

"I love your daddy," John said to me. "He saved my life."

The other friends told me the story:

"The Major calls him 'Big John,'" they said. "John's been bad to drink ever since he came home from the war, too. He was getting a little paycheck from the government, but his wife always got her hands on it before he did. She didn't want him drinking it up.

"But John could always find somebody to buy him a bottle, and his wife and daughter finally threw him out of the house. Know what he did? He went out in the woods and found an old, abandoned car. That's where he was living, in that old car.

"Somebody told the Major about him, so he went out there, got John and got him sobered up. He bought him something to eat and paid for him to get a room. The next Sunday, he brought John to church with him.

"Nobody could believe it. John hadn't looked that good in years. After church, we had dinner on the grounds and the Major asked everybody, 'Have you met my new friend, Big John?'

"John was like a child. He'd look up at the Major, and you could tell how much he loved and respected and appreciated him for helping.

"I never will forget those two eating chicken that day. I never saw two men go through as much fried chicken as they did after church.

"The Major would say, 'Big John, let's me and you have one more piece of that chicken.'

"John would say, 'Let's do it. Us old soldiers got to stick together.'

"John hasn't had a drink since and has been to church every Sunday. If the Major told him to run through a wall, he'd do it."

Daddy wasn't getting any better in the hospital. The doctor said it would be some time before he would know if there would be any permanent paralysis. Then, the doctor left town for a convention.

John came in one afternoon. Daddy had regained some consciousness. He complained mostly about the catheter. He begged the nurses to remove it.

"Get this thing out of me," he would plead.

When he opened his eyes, there was fear and pain in them. I sat by his bed for hours while he would drift off to troubled sleep. When he talked, it usually made no sense.

"He's out of his head," said John.

I didn't know whether to leave or stay. I wanted out of that hospital room, but I was afraid to go. I had no idea if he would be left permanently disabled. I didn't know what I would do with him if he was.

After the doctor had been gone three days, Big John came back and said, "We've got to get your daddy out of here. He's going to die if we don't. We need to get him up to the Veterans Hospital in Augusta. I was there, and they treat you real good. A man with his record ought to be in the Veterans Hospital where they can do him some good."

I knew what had happened. Daddy had told John about his war record, but he had not told him of his discharge that had been less than honorable. John did not know that Daddy was receiving no benefits from the army.

I didn't want to tell John the truth. I didn't want to strike down the image Big John had of him. But I was also beginning to agree with the assessment he had made of Daddy's condition. He certainly wasn't getting any better, and it seemed to both of us he was getting worse.

"All we got to do," John said, "is call up at the Veterans in Augusta, and they'll send an ambulance down to get him."

John said he would call. He wanted to know if I knew Daddy's service number. I said I didn't.

"It's probably in his wallet," John said.

I knew that it wasn't, but I decided to hire an ambulance in Metter, myself, and have Daddy taken to the hospital in Augusta. Then, I would have the attendant roll him into admissions and I would say only that he needed help, and that he had been in two wars, and that's all I would say I knew. I determined that when they saw his condition, they would treat him, and by the time they could get his records, maybe he would be well.

I called a local funeral home and hired the ambulance. They said it would cost me $50 to drive him to Augusta, eighty miles away.

I went to the nurses' station and told them I intended to remove Daddy from the hospital and take him to Augusta.

"Dr. [I forget his name] has to authorize that," a nurse said to me.

"When is he coming back?" I asked.

They weren't sure.

"If I don't get my daddy out of here," I said, "I think he's going to die, and I don't think you can stop me from taking him out."

The nurses said I would have to talk to the hospital administrator.

"If you want to remove your father, certainly you may," he said, "but we must make certain his bill is cleared before he leaves."

The bill was $400. "We were not able to determine whether or not your father had insurance," the man said. "We took him in because he was an emergency. Most hospitals won't do that anymore. We must insist someone pay the bill before he leaves."

I called my wife. I asked her how much we had in savings. We had $600.

"Put $400 in the checking account," I said.

"Why?"

"Because Daddy is going to die if I don't move him to another hospital, and I've got to pay his bill before they will let him go."

There was a silence.

"I told you I didn't want you giving him any of our money," she said.

"He's going to die if I don't," I said.

"I don't think it's right."

"It's all I can do."

"Doesn't he have brothers and sisters?"

"He's got me. That's all he's got. Put the goddamned money in the checking account."

She agreed reluctantly. When we later divorced, I told myself that one of the reasons I could get along just fine without her was that she didn't want me to spend money saving my father's life. I was rationalizing, of course. All she really knew of him was his past, and she didn't want him to take advantage of me. There was, in fact, cause for her concern. What she didn't know was that there was no part in me that would allow me to turn my back on him. He was my daddy, and I was all he had.

I wrote the check for the hospital bill. The ambulance people loaded Daddy in the back. I followed it to Augusta.

"You tell the Major I'll be up to see him soon as I can," said John as we drove away.

My plan worked to perfection. I had the attendant roll Daddy into admissions when we arrived in Augusta. I didn't know if the federal government might arrest me for fraud, but at the time it didn't seem that important.

I told admissions his name and that he lived in Savannah and that he had fought in World War II and in Korea and that he had Purple Hearts and a Bronze Star for valor. When they asked for his service number, I said I had no idea what it was and that he didn't have it on his person.

They called down a doctor. The doctor examined Daddy. He told a nurse to get a room ready for him. I gave the doctor all the information I had about Daddy's health and condition.

"He looks like a very sick man," the doctor said.

I was at the hospital several more hours. After tests and further examination, the doctor explained what had happened to Daddy and said that his chances of survival were very good, but, as I had been told earlier, there might be some permanent paralysis.

I remember feeling concerned, of course, but I also remember suddenly feeling very adult. I had handled a major crisis. I had, with John's help, saved my daddy's life. I was tough under pressure.

I drove back to Atlanta that night. When I got home, my wife met me at the door.

"I think he's going to live," I said.

She said she was glad. We always slept closely, but that night, I turned my back to her. I was playing the lonely martyr. It was me and Daddy against the world now. I felt as close to him as I ever had.

CHAPTER
14

THEY TRIED TO MAKE DADDY PAY WHEN HE WAS RELEASED from the Veterans Hospital in Augusta. He was three weeks in recovering from the stroke. There had been no permanent paralysis.

They had discovered he wasn't eligible for veteran's army benefits and they wanted him to pay. He simply told them the truth, that he didn't have any money. He also told them a lie. He said he would pay off the bill in installments. My daddy had no intention of doing that.

Then, they hit on me. The hospital wrote me a letter saying that since I was the one who had brought my father in, I was liable for the bill. I totally ignored the letter. I never heard anything else.

Daddy went back to the Savannah area and got the last job he would ever have, teaching school at one of those private Christian academies.

"Mahvelous job, just mahvelous," he described it to me over the phone.

A few months later, he married for the third time. He met this lady at church, a widow. She took him home and cooked him a meal, and he asked her to marry him and she agreed.

She lived in Pembroke, Georgia, thirty or so miles west of Savannah. It was a tiny village with a Methodist Church, which is all Daddy needed to quickly become a legend in any small community. They called his wife "Aunt Dolly." She was in her seventies when she married "the Major," as she quickly learned to call him.

"Your father has done a wonderful thing," he said to me over the phone, announcing his marriage. "I have just met the most mahvelous woman, and we have married. You must come and meet her. Her name is Aunt Dolly, and she fries the most wonderful chicken on earth."

My wife didn't want to go, so I left Atlanta on a Friday afternoon on the *Nancy Hanks* train.

"Buy a ticket for Dover," Daddy had said.

"That's a town?"

"Not much of one," he said, "but the train will stop there if there is anybody getting on or getting off."

Dover was a falling-down depot and a light, but Daddy and Aunt Dolly were there to meet me.

We drove back to their house in Pembroke and Aunt Dolly fried a chicken. Daddy called her "Mother."

I liked her. She was a dignified lady. She lived in a house that had been in her family for years. It had a front porch and a rocking chair. After the chicken, we went out to the front porch. Daddy sat in the rocker and told stories. Aunt Dolly sat in her chair and hung on his every word. All we needed was for Barney to drop by and we would have been a scene out of Andy Griffith and Mayberry.

Saturday, Daddy and I drove into Savannah.

"I have some mahvelous friends here," he said. "I want them to meet you."

We went to a restaurant. Daddy knew a man there.

"This is my son, Lewis Jr.," he introduced me. "He's a writer for the Atlanta newspapers. That's how I get to visit him. I buy the paper every day and we visit."

We went into another restaurant. Daddy often was a two-lunch man.

"Wonderful food here, just wonderful," Daddy rolled on.

On the way back from Savannah, we talked.

"I like Aunt Dolly," I said.

"Mahvelous person" was the reply I knew I would get.

"Do you love her?" I asked.

"Love her, love her, love her! She is a delightful individual."

"Daddy, you're getting older. You need a place to settle down."

"You are absolutely correct, son, and I think I have found my new bailiwick with Aunt Dolly in Pembroke."

"It would really make me happy if you would stay here."

"I intend to, son. I am going to make my new home here, and I want you to come and visit anytime that you can. I told Aunt Dolly that one of the conditions of our marriage was my son could come and visit anytime he wanted to. She agreed wholeheartedly."

The scars of the earlier stroke, I hoped, might make Daddy even more determined to settle. And he had to be tired of the life he had been living since leaving the army.

I often wondered how many mornings he awakened not knowing where he would sleep that night. He must have been in thousands of motels and cheap boardinghouses. And then, there were all those homes for wayfarers who had trouble with the drink.

He often traveled without a suitcase. That was because he often had nothing to put in it.

The older I became, the more sad his life appeared to me. He had his career in the army. He was a hero, almost worshipped by his men. And he had landed a post-Korea station as the Fort Benning athletic officer. I knew how much he loved coaching.

He had a wife who loved him. He had a son. He was on a mountain when he fell. He could have done anything, been anything. I remain convinced.

I remember conversations between him and Mother when he first returned from Korea and began making speeches across the state. They talked of his retiring from the army at some point, possibly to enter politics.

The man was born to be a politician. He was a

brilliant speaker, a conniver, a man who drew instant respect, a man who could meet you one moment and convince you to cosign a note with him at your bank the next.

"When I think of all your daddy gave up," my mother used to say, shaking her head.

He remains as unique an individual as I ever met and the last ten years of my life have been spent searching out characters. Certainly, he could have been a politician. A preacher. An entertainer. He was the Amazing Mr. Pennypacker, a Houdini for his disappearing acts, a Jackie Gleason for his robust appearance and zest.

He was as much at home around a bum as he was a corporate executive. It was impossible to ignore him. He commanded each room he walked into, and every conversation.

I never saw him angry. I saw him hurt and I saw him crying, but I never saw him lose his temper. He was a joy to be around. People flocked to him. He was the Snellville Svengali. Even when you knew he was telling you a lie, you wanted so much to believe him, you hoped by some miracle it might be the truth, after all.

He was a handsome man. When his hair turned gray, late in his life, it gave him an unmistakable aura of distinction. When he was down and out, he was down and out. But when he was up, his shoes were always shined, his hair always cut to military length, his clothes always clean and pressed.

Women loved him. His mistake probably was not taking as much advantage of them as he could have. Women wanted to marry him, wanted to give him a home, wanted to shower him with gifts, wanted simply to be in his presence.

His story is tragic for what might have been.

Maybe he did give it a good try with Aunt Dolly in Pembroke, but the inevitable did finally occur. Six or so months after they married, I got a call from the Dempsey Hotel in Macon. The Dempsey was one of Daddy's favorite places to drink himself into oblivion for three or four days.

He was in the hotel and drunk, they said. He had spent all his money on liquor and if I didn't want them to call the police, I should come get him.

I always remember how those rooms smelled when I went to get him off a bender. It was a sickening smell of stale booze, mixed with sweat and how a body smells when it screams out for a bath. Go to any mission for the homeless, any haunt where winos sleep it off, and you will know that smell.

I drove down to Macon, got him halfway sober and then made him take a shower. His clothes were putrid. I took his only shirt to a one-hour cleaners. I had his suit pressed. I brought him some coffee and something to eat.

"Don't hate me," he said. Again.

I asked him if Aunt Dolly knew where he was. He said she didn't. I called her.

"I can't live with him if he is going to do things like this," she said. "My children would never allow me to live with a man who drinks."

This is not just anybody who drinks, I wanted to say to her. This is a man falling even more deeply into an abyss from which he one day will not be able to crawl out.

Instead, I tried to convince her to give him another chance.

I didn't know what to do with him otherwise. I certainly couldn't take him home to Atlanta and my wife in that condition.

But I couldn't turn him out on the streets, either. I had made that pact with myself when I realized I was the only one left in his life who hadn't totally given up on him, or was at least on the brink of it, as his wife certainly was.

Aunt Dolly said he could come home if he was sober and promised not to drink anymore. I knew I could get him sober and I knew he could promise not to drink anymore. He had done it hundreds of times before.

I bought him a bus ticket home.

"Daddy, I can't keep doing this," I said to him before his bus left.

"I know I'm being an embarrassment to you," he said.

"It's not that," I went on, "it's just that I've got a job and a wife of my own, and I can't keep bailing you out of these situations."

"I'll be better," he said. He was like a child promising not to get into the cookie jar again.

And he was childlike. Now that I had come of age, our roles had switched. He was the child, the little boy who had a difficult time taking care of himself, and I was the protector of his well-being, as much of it as I could protect.

There was no more Daddy in his uniform, with

his campaign stripes showing proudly on his chest. No more Daddy taking me to the movies and answering all my questions. Now he was a broken-down old man, and I was all that was holding up his last legs.

I never shared this with anybody. I wasn't that close to the remaining relatives on his side. I didn't want to worry my mother. She also probably would have said something like, "Let him get out of his own troubles." I didn't talk to my wife that much about him anymore, either. I knew how she felt about him, and how her feeling that way angered me, and we were having enough problems without adding yet another.

I soon came to realize Daddy probably wasn't going to live that much longer. I remembered the old people talking at home about people who'd had strokes.

"They might get through that first one," they would say, "but hardly anybody makes it through a second one."

Daddy had a history of high blood pressure, and he already had had that first stroke. He had looked awful that day in Macon. I could see the sickness in him.

When I was a kid, I would wonder how it would feel for my daddy to die. I remembered looking at Mike Murphy when his daddy, Mr. Red, died. It was a horrible thought to have. I tried to avoid it.

But as shameful as it might sound, I began to wonder if it wouldn't be best for both of us if he died. Life held so little promise for him anymore. There would be no settling down, no straightening out. For however long he lived, he would be the same as he had been.

And how much longer before he became an even greater burden for me? How many more Dempsey Hotels would there be? What if I had to put him in some sort of home?

I began to wonder if I was turning on him too. Was my daddy too much trouble for me now? Was I going to turn away from him as everybody else had done?

I began to dread his calls. As soon as I heard his voice, I could tell instantly whether or not he had been drinking. I always felt a great sense of relief when his first words were out and I could determine his sobriety.

Daddy got his job back at the school, amazingly enough, following the last Dempsey Hotel experience. And Aunt Dolly welcomed him back, too. I even visited them again. Took the *Nancy Hanks* and got off at Dover. Ate some more of Aunt Dolly's fried chicken. Sat out on the porch and rocked.

But Daddy lasted only a few more months. One morning, he phoned me at work. I was up to my ears with the first edition.

"Hello there, Lewis Jr.!" he began. He was drinking. My heart sank. And I was angry. He had no business bothering me at work, especially at this time of the morning when the world was already caving in around me.

I asked him where he was.

"The Americana Hotel."

"You're in Atlanta?"

"Came in on the *Nancy Hanks* yesterday. Mahvelous train. Just mahvelous."

"Daddy, I'm busy as hell trying to get out the first edition."

"I don't mean to be a nuisance, son," he said.

"Do you need anything?"

"Not a thing."

"Have you been drinking?"

"Just one or two. I'm not having anymore, though. I'm seeing a man about a job."

"Call me back, later," I said. "I don't have time to talk right now."

I called the hotel again in a couple of hours. He didn't answer the phone. I called again. Still no answer. I left work, and walked to the Americana, a few blocks from the newspaper. I got his room number at the desk and went up and knocked on his door. There was still no sign of life inside.

Maybe he had stopped drinking and was keeping his appointment, I thought. Who was I kidding? I asked a maid to unlock the door.

There he was on the bed, snoring. There was that smell again. I wanted to hit him. I wanted to scream at him. At that moment, I hated him. I had never felt that way before.

But I had my job now. I had to catch a flight later that afternoon to cover a ball game in New Orleans. This was my life. This is what I had wanted to do for so long. Now I was doing it, and here he was interfering.

I shook him. He didn't wake up. Shades of the Birmingham Motel. I checked his wallet. He had no money.

I tried the cold towel trick on him as Bob had done. This time, fortunately, he wasn't so far gone that he didn't respond. I made him sit up on the end of the bed.

"Son," he said, "do you think you could get me a little drink?"

"Hell, no," I said. "You're supposed to be seeing a man about a job, remember?"

"I don't want a job. I want a drink. *Please* get me a drink."

He was begging. He was a pitiful old drunk begging his son for a drink.

I continued to refuse. He continued to beg.

"In the name of God, son," he said, "just get me one drink and I'll feel better."

I held my ground.

"I've got to catch a plane," I said. "Just what in hell should I do with you? You don't have any money."

"I'll get some."

I was close to panicking. I knew if I simply left him, he would find a means of getting money. He was a genius without peer when it came to that. But he would just get drunker and drunker and when I got back from New Orleans, he would still be in the hotel, and I would wind up paying his bill.

The bus station was across the street from the hotel.

"If I bought you a bus ticket home, would Aunt Dolly take you back in?" I asked him.

"Yes, yes," he said.

"Here is what we're going to do. You're going to get dressed and we're going to walk out through the lobby and over to the bus station. I don't want you to make a sound in the lobby. Try to walk as straight as possible. I don't want the front desk to see you and ask me to pay your bill. Do you understand that?"

"I can't have a drink?"

"No, you can't have a drink."

"Don't hate me," he said, beginning to cry. This was all I needed.

"I don't hate you, Daddy," I said, "but you've got to leave here."

"I've never heard you talk like this to me before," he said.

"I've got to talk to you this way."

"You're my son."

"That doesn't matter, Daddy. I've got a job and a wife, and I've got to catch a plane."

"I have cancer."

"What?"

"I went to see a doctor and he said I have a cancer."

"You can't mean that."

"He said I have a cancer and I'm not going to live very long."

I was stunned.

"I'm sorry, Daddy," was all I could get out.

"I don't want to die and not see you anymore."

"I don't want you to die, either, Daddy."

"There is nothing they can do."

"You're not sure of that."

"Yes, I am."

There was a pause. I was still in shock.

"Son," Daddy said, "you wouldn't deprive a dying man of a drink, would you?"

Damn. He would say anything for a drink.

"Get dressed," I said to him.

I held him as we walked through the lobby of the hotel. He tended to lean a bit to starboard, but I got him out of there without anybody seeing us. I made him sit in the waiting room of the bus station while I went to buy him a ticket to Pembroke.

There was a bus leaving for Macon in forty-five minutes. He would have an hour's wait there before changing buses. I paid for the ticket, knowing full well that the chance he would not get off in Macon and head straight to the Dempsey was slim, indeed, but all I wanted was to get him out of Atlanta.

I then became concerned the driver would not allow him on the bus if he noticed he was drunk. What on earth would I do if I couldn't get him on the bus? I made him drink two cups of coffee.

When his bus was called for boarding, I walked him to it. I gave him the ticket and told him he had to change in Macon. He hadn't begged for a drink since we left the hotel. I felt better because of that.

He got past the bus driver fine. I walked with him and put him into a seat near the back. I put the remainder of the ticket in his coat pocket. I had some advance cash for my trip to New Orleans. I put $10 in his wallet.

"Go home," I said to him. "And don't spend this money on something to drink when you get to Macon. There won't be anybody to come take care of you."

"Home. I'll go straight home," he said.

"You really don't have a cancer, do you, Daddy?" I asked him.

He wrinkled his brow and pooched out his lips in a comical way and said, "The war didn't get me, and neither will cancer."

I watched the bus leave the station with him in it. I drove to the airport and caught my flight to New Orleans. After I checked into my hotel, I called my wife.

"Your daddy just called," she said.

"What?"

"He said he was in East Point."

"That's impossible. I put him on a bus to Macon. East Point's the first stop out of Atlanta."

"All I know," she continued, "is he called from East Point and said he was in town for a job interview."

"Did he sound drunk?"

"A little."

"Did he ask you to come get him?"

"No, but he promised to bring me a new dress the next time he saw me."

If he hadn't asked her to come get him and hadn't asked her for money, I figured that somewhere on that bus from Atlanta to East Point, perhaps a fifteen-minute ride, he obviously had come into some additional funds. God, I wish I could have heard the story he used on a fellow passenger, or even the bus driver, for that matter.

I called Aunt Dolly's on Monday to see if he was there. He was. He sounded fine.

"How was your ball game in New Orleans?" he asked.

"Why did you get off the bus?" I snapped.

"I met the most wonderful man who insisted I get off the bus with him at East Point and go have dinner with him and his family. His wife cooked us the most mahvelous dinner and they had a piano and she played so well."

"Did you play?"

"A few selections," he answered.

"What a waste of talent" is something else my mother used to say about him.

CHAPTER
15

DADDY DIED AUGUST 12, 1970. HE WAS FIFTY-SIX. I WAS twenty-three.

Aunt Dolly called me a week earlier to tell me Daddy was drinking again.

"He started drinking last week and wouldn't quit. I said, 'Major, I don't allow drinking in my house. My children just wouldn't stand for it.'

"He said he didn't care about my children, that he was going to drink. I tried to take his bottle away from him, and he threatened me. I just don't know about anything like that, so I called the sheriff and he came and got him."

"Is he in jail?" I asked.

"I don't know," she said. "That was last night. I haven't heard anything from him since."

I called the sheriff's office.

"We just kept him overnight," I was told. "He got out this morning. I don't know where he went."

He went to Claxton. He started drinking again. He was walking down a street in Claxton when he collapsed.

Some people saw him fall. They called the police, who came and tried to revive him. They said he had bruises on his head, as if someone had hit him.

The policeman took him to the hospital. How the hospital found me was from the letter I had written him. It was in his jacket pocket. He had no identification. He had no money.

A nurse called me in Atlanta and said a man had been admitted to the hospital carrying a letter that had my name and address on the envelope. I identified him as my father and asked what the matter with him was. She said he had a stroke and that he was in critical condition.

My wife and I had only recently separated. I was still in our house. I called Uncle John Wesley, Daddy's brother. He said he would ride with me to Claxton. It was a four-hour drive from Atlanta.

We got in at two in the morning. The night nurse let us into Daddy's room. She said he was in a semicoma, whatever that is. I saw the bruises on his face and head. I knew he was going to die.

Uncle John Wesley and I checked into a motel. I called Aunt Dolly in Pembroke to tell her where Daddy was.

"My daughter is driving in from California to take me away," she said.

"You're not coming to the hospital?" I asked her. She said she wasn't.

I told her I thought Daddy was dying.

"My daughter told me not to go near the Major again," she said sadly.

I asked if she knew anything about the bruises on Daddy's head and face.

"I think he slipped in the tub," she said.

We stayed in Claxton with Daddy for four days. There was no change in his condition. He remained unconscious. The doctor said the stroke had been massive. I asked about the bruises.

"We think he probably got them when he fell from the stroke," the doctor said.

Uncle John Wesley said it looked like somebody had beaten him up.

"He probably got drunk and somebody rolled him for whatever money he had," was his explanation.

After the four days, we realized there was nothing more we could do at the hospital. Uncle John Wesley, then in his late sixties, needed to get back to work.

"I still mess with a few old used cars now and then," he said.

We drove back through a rainstorm. I had never been close to my uncle. I liked him, though. He always wore a big hat and smoked one Camel after another. His fingers were yellow from the several thousand miles of smoke that had passed over them.

He was a wise old man who lived into his eighties. He became the quintessential Grizzard to me. He was big, like all the Grizzards. He had his own brand of wit, dryer than my father's but perhaps more thoughtful.

"I never sold a car to a man who didn't deserve it," he said once.

On the way back to Atlanta he said what I had wanted to say. He said something that took away any guilt I had thinking death was the only hope Daddy had left. Uncle John Wesley said, "He don't deserve no more hell."

I kept in touch with the hospital after I returned home. Three days after I returned, the night nurse awakened me with a call. It was shortly after five in the morning.

"Your daddy's worse," she said.

"How bad is it?" I asked.

"You'd better come."

I drove Interstate 75 South toward Macon, ninety miles from Atlanta. The drive took me just over an hour. I left Macon on I-16 toward Savannah. The interstate ended near Soperton. I took the two-lane as fast as I dared on into Claxton. I made the 200-mile drive in just over three hours.

There were three men in the hospital room with Daddy when I arrived. They were friends from his church in Pembroke.

They stood at one end of his bed. Each had his hands folded in front of him. Country folk deal with death quietly. They do not fight it, generally. They are at peace with its inevitability. Their faith, forged in them for a lifetime, makes acceptance of death a ritual of calm and dignity.

"I'm Daddy's son," I said to them.

"Yes sir," one of the old men said. "The Major was always talking about you. He was very proud of you."

I was struck by their respectful stance toward me. All three men were much older than I, but their upbringing had taught them reverence for the family of the dying.

"Has the doctor been in?" I wanted to know.

"Came in just a while ago," one of the men said. "The Major has pneumonia."

He was blue. My daddy was blue. Each breath came with obvious labor.

"The doctor said he could go at any time," another of the men said.

So this was it. He would die in this bed, in this tiny hospital in this town with his son and three friends to watch him go.

I wanted to tell the three men his life story. I wanted them to know more of what they were seeing pass into the ages before them.

They knew only "the Major," a big, happy man with a thousand stories.

"Your daddy was a blessing to our community and church," one of them said.

Tell me about it, I thought. He sang and played for you, didn't he? And he made you laugh for a time and forget your troubles. He wasn't like other men you knew. His personality was so forceful. He brought life to wherever he happened to be.

But you don't know all the story, I wanted to say. You don't know how brave he was. You don't know how he led men into battle. You don't know how many nights he spent doubting there would be another for him. You don't know about the hell in Korea, about the years of loneliness and wandering. You don't know my mother and how much he loved her. You don't know about the torment that followed him. You don't know there must be some black secret that is dying with him.

You don't know how he was when I was a little boy. How I cried for him when we thought he was lost, how we cried for him when he came back to us.

You don't know what a terrible waste you are witnessing. This was a special man, a gifted man, a man for whom there could have been no limit to his accomplishments.

But look at him. Death should not be inglorious for such a man. Better had he died heroically, felled in battle.

A nurse came into the room and checked his pulse. He is just a body to her, I thought, an aging, sputtering machine that she is monitoring for its inevitable passage into obsolescence.

I looked out of the window. The morning was steaming. I remembered how much he had hated hot weather. I remembered all the ice water I saw him drink.

He would pour it into his mouth in great gulps, and then when he had taken the glass away from his mouth he would roar, "What a mahvelous glass of water!" I almost laughed at the remembrance.

I thought of that voice, that magnificent voice and the way he used it as a tool. No man could talk like my daddy could talk. He spoke in symphonic overtures, this man. I imagined him suddenly opening his eyes and booming, "In the name of God, son, what on earth is happening here!"

I had vowed not to cry. This was another test of

my manhood, another in a series of tests I was constantly giving myself, for no other reason than to prove my manhood in Daddy's sight. To cry now would be a sign of my weakness. To cry now would be to disavow my adulthood. I stood there alone with my dying father. There was no mother to turn to and bury my face against for comfort. This was mine.

He continued to struggle for each breath. I thought each he took would be his last, but after a grueling pause, there would be another. The blue in his face was deepening.

The silence is deafening at a death watch. I wanted some great and furious words to say. But none came. The three men were also silent. They obviously felt to speak and interrupt my grief would have been terribly out of place.

The last breath came. We all saw it and heard it. There was a sense of relieved sigh to it. Or maybe there wasn't. Maybe that was my imagination.

Seconds passed. Then, a minute was gone. I put my daddy's hand in mine. I held it tightly. Another minute passed. I would not speak. I knew I would not speak. Someone else would have to signal the end.

"I believe your daddy has passed," one of the men said.

I closed my eyes and held his hand. One of the men slipped out of the room. He came back with the nurse.

She took Daddy's other hand and checked for a pulse. She looked up at me and found my eyes. She said nothing to me, but her eyes were the messenger.

"I'll get the doctor," she said.

I continued to hold Daddy's hand.

The doctor came in. He put a stethoscope to Daddy's chest and listened.

"He's gone," the doctor said to me. The nurse pulled the sheet over Daddy's head. I still held onto his hand.

The nurse and the doctor left the room. One of the men walked toward me and put his arm around me.

"If it would be all right with you," he said, "I think we should have a word of prayer."

I nodded yes. The man prayed. I didn't shut my eyes. I kept staring at the form under the sheet. When the prayer was over, the men said if there was anything they could do. . . . I thanked them for coming. They left the room.

I stood over the body, with Daddy's hand still in mine. I was dazed. I thought of trumpets. I wanted trumpets, goddammit! I wanted the pealing of bells. I wanted something more than the silence.

The helplessness I felt became immense. This is it, I thought. It is over and it had been so quiet, so lacking of drama. He breathed and then he didn't breathe anymore, and the nurses came and the doctor came and they pulled a sheet over his head and a man had said a prayer. That had been it. Death is a sneaking son-of-a-bitch. It makes not a sound.

After a time, probably seconds, maybe an hour, I let Daddy's hand drop beside him. The momentum of the drop caused it to swing for a moment, and then it stilled. I pulled the sheet back just enough to put the hand and arm underneath it. I thought of pulling the sheet back and looking one last time at his face. I didn't.

I walked out of the room. There were immediate realities to confront. I signed a couple of things. I don't know what.

There was the matter of the hospital bill. I expected that. What I didn't expect was that it would have to be paid in total—$800—before the hospital would release the body. I spoke of that situation earlier. A call to Jim Minter and the matter was settled. Jim said he was sorry. He said to take all the time I needed before coming back to work. I have called Jim first in the midst of many more crises since. He is my voice of strength and reason.

I called my mother next.

"Daddy died," I said.

"He did," she replied, with an amount of sorrow in her voice.

"I loved him," I said.

"I know you did," she replied.

I called Bob. I called Uncle John Wesley. He said he would call a friend he had at a funeral home and make the necessary arrangements.

The doctor suggested I call a local funeral home to have Daddy's body returned to Atlanta. The man there was very nice. He said he would pick up the body in an hour and have it back in Atlanta by late afternoon. I was struck by the way the body had become an "it."

One of the men in the room, the one who had

prayed, was still in the hospital. He asked if I needed anything.

"Lunch," I said. I suddenly felt hunger.

I followed the man to his house. His wife prepared a meal. They talked again about how much they thought of the Major.

I called my estranged wife at work from their house. I needed her.

"Just come home," I said, "until the funeral is over."

She said she would be at the house when I got there.

I went back to the hospital after lunch. There were more papers to sign. The nurse gave me a plastic bag with Daddy's personal effects. They included a suit, a shirt, a tie, socks and shoes, and underwear. Boxer shorts. There was a wallet, which had nothing inside it. Nothing. There was a ring. A cheap ring. There was a watch. The glass cover was out.

As I was walking out of the hospital, Aunt Dolly walked in. She was with another woman.

"This is my daughter," Aunt Dolly said.

The woman didn't speak. She scowled at me.

"Daddy's dead," I said.

"I was called," Aunt Dolly said.

"I'm taking my mother away," the daughter said, still scowling.

I asked if I could go by Aunt Dolly's house and pick up Daddy's other belongings.

The daughter looked at Aunt Dolly and scowled her disapproval.

Aunt Dolly said, "By all means."

Back at her house, she put Daddy's things in a cardboard box. There were a couple of suits and shirts and socks and underwear. And then I saw the red baseball cap and the whistle he had been wearing that day ten years earlier when he appeared at my first high-school basketball game.

They looked so much like him. The hat was tattered and the whistle was rusty, but I could see him so clearly in my mind in that hat, with the whistle around his neck. The emotion welled inside me. I fought back the tears.

"You know your father threatened my mother," the daughter said.

I shrugged.

"It's over," I said.

I put the box in the trunk of my car and drove toward Atlanta. I never saw or heard from Aunt Dolly again. She didn't come to the funeral.

As I drove home slowly, I did begin to feel some relief. I told myself that at least he hadn't suffered. I had heard people say things like that before. And there would be no more calls, no more trips to the Dempsey. No more worrying about what to do with my daddy, where to take him, how to sneak him out of a hotel without having to pay his bill.

Some guilt came back. My daddy had just died and I was relieved because he wouldn't be causing me any more trouble. But at least I had stayed with him until the end. I never had not been there when he needed me, even if it meant arguments with my wife, days off from work, and countless embarrassments and discomforts.

But maybe I hadn't done enough. Maybe I should

have moved him to another hospital this time, too. Maybe there was somebody who had beaten him up and caused his stroke. Maybe I should go back and talk to the police and find out if there was someone responsible for my daddy's death.

But what could I do? I was only twenty-three. The police wouldn't want to launch some investigation that probably would lead nowhere for some kid whose daddy got drunk, had a stroke, fell down, and then died when his lungs quit working. I was just trying to be dramatic here. I refused to believe Daddy just up and died. I wanted there to be more for him in death. I wanted his death to be more special than just another man stops breathing.

And wasn't I that way about everything? Didn't I always want things to be more special, more dramatic? Didn't my friends always say, "Grizzard, you aren't ever satisfied"?

My entire life had been like that. I wanted everything to have sparklers on it. I hated the routine, the everyday. Trumpets. I always wanted goddamned trumpets.

My wife had cleaned the house and had made supper when I arrived home. She held me. She said she knew how much I had loved my daddy. She said she was sorry that he died.

I remember writing something about Daddy that night. I hardly remember what I wrote, however, and the piece has long since been lost. I remember the theme of it, though. It was that a great man had died, and I was the only one who had any real sense of his greatness.

That is probably where this book had its subconscious conception. That feeling of frustration, that nobody but me really knew the big picture, never left me after that night.

Nobody was taking this thing hard enough, I thought. There should have been wailing and gnashing of teeth. But who was to do it?

Certainly not my mother. It simply had been too long. Uncle John Wesley was a man who took everything in his stride. Betty had done all she could have done when she was married to Daddy. Bob loved him, but he was not a man to carry on. Aunt Dolly was on her way someplace with her scowling daughter. My wife was just doing me a favor being with me.

Daddy and his memory were mine. His curse was mine. I had endured a lifetime of it. Of all the people he had touched, he had touched me the deepest. He had become my burden in life. He would be my burden in death. Seventeen years later, what am I saying here?

I am saying, know this man and what he was. Know what he gave and know that he got too little in return. I cry for my daddy. I want somebody else to cry for him, too. This book is my gift to his memory. These are the tears that didn't come when I held his hand in death.

I would do his funeral differently if I had it to do over again because—and here is that frustration once more—it had no flair, no connection with the sort of life he lived.

Uncle John Wesley picked out the funeral home. He and my Aunt Rufy and I picked out the casket. Uncle John Wesley also found a preacher to perform the services. I didn't know the man. He hadn't known my father.

The paper called the next morning after his death. They wanted some information for the obituary. I said that he was a veteran and had been a coach and teacher.

It was funny, that the headline that appeared on his obit was a 1–0, the same sort of headline that was the first I had written my first day at the *Journal.* It said:

L. M. GRIZZARD,
COACH, DIES

The obit was five paragraphs long.

I wanted a flag for the casket. I looked up a number in the telephone book for the Veterans Administration and I called and asked if they gave flags for the funerals of former soldiers. A woman said they didn't.

Uncle John Wesley said I should call the Veterans of Foreign Wars in Snellville.

"Your daddy used to drink with some of those ol' boys," he said.

I talked to a man at the VFW who said, "I've known Lewis all my life." He said there would be a flag and there would be an honor guard of VFW members at the funeral if I wanted such a thing. I said I did.

We had the funeral in the funeral home chapel. The preacher came over to me as I stood in front of Daddy's casket and asked a few questions about his life.

"I always like to personalize a funeral service," he said.

I said what I always said. I said he'd been in two wars and that he was a great singer and piano player and that people enjoyed hearing him tell stories.

"Your uncle told me about his singing," the preacher, who wore a shiny suit and had a moustache, said. "I'm going to do a song."

Mostly, the preacher read from the Bible. I don't remember the name of the song. Here is what I would have done differently:

I would have located Reverend Gilbert Steadham to do the service. Reverend Steadham was minister at the Moreland Methodist Church when Daddy came home from Korea. He had been very kind to my mother and me during the time Daddy was gone. When he heard of Daddy's troubles in Fort Benning, he had tried to help all he could. I didn't think of Reverend Steadham until after the funeral was over.

I would have somebody deliver a eulogy. Had I thought I could have gotten through it, I would have done it myself. I wish now I had asked Bob to deliver a eulogy. If any man needed one to be read at his funeral, it was my daddy.

I would have had more music and I would have had better music. I would have found a girl singer somewhere and she would have sung "It Is No Secret."

It is no secret
What God can do.

What he's done for others,
He'll do for you.
With arms wide open,
He'll pardon you,
It is no secret,
What God can do.

I would have had somebody blow "Taps."

We took him back to his home church in Snellville to bury him in the graveyard at Zoar Methodist. There was a plot available next to his mother. Aunt Rufy said she wanted him to have it.

"Mother loved Lewis so much," she said.

My wife sat next to me in the front row under the tent at the graveside services. Uncle John Wesley and Aunt Rufy and her husband, Uncle Harry, sat with me.

Bob was a pallbearer. I had requested that. Uncle John Wesley knew some other men who had known Daddy in Snellville. They were the other pallbearers.

My mother was there with H.B. Betty came. Minter was there. So were others from the *Journal* sports staff.

The men from the VFW lined up behind the casket. They wore their VFW caps. When the preacher had finished his final prayer, two of the men from the VFW walked to the casket and folded the flag. One of them handed it to me.

That was when I finally lost it. I held that flag in my hands, and the significance of it tore me in half. I buried my face in it and I cried hard and long. My wife put her arms around me.

I couldn't stop the sobbing. I felt the anger and the sadness and the frustration all at once. I was angry that I felt so alone in this. Why weren't the others feeling the pain I felt? Why did they seem much less cognizant of this man's worth than I was?

And, God, the sadness here. An old soldier is dead. A great soldier is dead. And in a tiny church-yard, he goes to rest beside his mother, who loved him so much, as his son cries his heart out.

I couldn't make anybody understand all this. I didn't have the words, the power to explain it. The frustration was that this was the end. The story would go untold in its entirety.

Mother and H.B. and my wife and I went for something to eat after the funeral. Afterwards they went home to Moreland, and my wife and I went back to the house. I had slept very little in three days. We went to bed early. I went to sleep in her arms.

When I awakened the next morning, she had gone back to her apartment. She had washed my clothes before she left. It was Saturday. I called a friend. We went to Underground Atlanta that night, and I got drunk. When I started crying about my daddy, my friend drove me back to his apartment and put me to bed.

The next day, I went back to the house and packed my clothes. I moved in with my friend. I sold the house several weeks later.

I go back sometimes and stand over Daddy's grave.

CHAPTER
16

SOME YEARS AGO, MY STEPBROTHER, BOB HANSON, BE-
came Ludlow Porch. He is Atlanta's favorite radio
talk-show host. He is a sought-after speaker. He is
the author of four hilarious books.

I write a syndicated newspaper column in which I
at least attempt to be humorous. I've spent a lot of
time behind an after-dinner dais myself. This is my
eighth book.

We both are still stealing Daddy's material. We
both owe him dearly for the success we have had in
our careers. He inspired our brand of humor. We
both know that and accept that and are proud of
the influence he has had upon us.

When we are together, we tell and retell the stories. If we are drinking, I usually wind up in tears.
Ludlow understands.

Bob—Ludlow—has said it often: "Wouldn't it be
wonderful if we still had him? Wouldn't he be

proud of us? We could set him up with a nice place to live, hire somebody to look after him, and just enjoy him."

Yeah. And just enjoy him. I daydream about that sometimes. I wish my daddy could read one of my columns. Hear me make a speech. Listen to the inflections of my voice in which I imitate him. I wish he could read this book. It says what I did not know how to say to him when he was alive.

There will never be another day in my life that passes without my having at least one thought of him. I hear a story, and it reminds me of him. I hear a word or a phrase he used. I get letters from people who see my name in a newspaper or on a book and write to ask if I am related to the Lewis Grizzard they think they went to school with, or the Lewis Grizzard who taught them in school.

I once received a letter from a woman in Kentucky who said Daddy had coached her son in basketball at Fort Benning. She said he had been very kind to her son and that he and the team once had stayed at her house on a road trip to play a team from a Kentucky post.

"We brought in cots for the boys to sleep. How they loved your father. He was so nice to our son. He borrowed $300 from my husband before he left. We never got it back, but we wanted him to have it for what he did for our boy." That's my daddy.

I was doing a book autographing in Birmingham once. A man came up to me and took my hand and held it tightly. He said, "The last time I saw your daddy, we were fightin' Krauts in Belgium."

A few years later, I was on a boat taking a cruise

down the Rhine River through Germany. Several veterans were on the boat, returning to see what they had left as servicemen in 1945.

There was a one-armed Texan who was shot down during an air raid over Germany. There was a Canadian who drove a tank from Normandy to Berlin. We were at a table in the ship's bar one night. The Texan and the Canadian told their stories. I told my father's. I told how the war had left him. How I held it to blame for ruining his life and, eventually, for killing him.

There was an old German at our table. He spoke only a little English. He had said he had once been held prisoner by the Americans during the war and that they had treated him well.

When he heard my father's story, when he saw my tears, he put his arms around me and said, "Forgive. You must forgive." I never answered him.

I see my father in myself more than I do anywhere else, however. Some of my friends have said they worry about the fact I often emulate him. They say they do not want to see me come to the same end as my father. I don't think I will go that far. I have his three marriages behind me, but I do not want to know the pain he tried to wash down in all those benders.

I look around me now that this project is coming to an end. My desk is cluttered with my notes. There are clips of old newspapers all over the floor. The papers from Daddy's record packet are scattered about. Once I am finished here, I will put them back into a safe place, and, on occasion, I will bring them out and look at them again after a time.

There were some pictures in the packet, too. There is one of me in my baseball outfit, standing next to my daddy on the Fort Benning bench during the game. He is wearing a white Ben Hogan golf hat, a short-sleeved shirt, a pair of white pants and a pair of two-tone shoes. The man was a sport. I plan to have some of the pictures framed. Maybe I will do a montage and hang it on the wall, next to Daddy's Bronze Star and Purple Hearts, which I had framed years ago.

This book is on its third typewriter. The "E" character came off the first typewriter I used. The ribbon stopped returning on another. That is something I believe in, typewriters. I didn't write one line of this book on one of those word processor gizmos. A man should not write the story of his daddy on anything that has to be plugged in.

Writing this book has been a draining experience. I have relived so many memories, so many good ones and so many bad ones. But I am proud that I have done it. It has been worth the effort, because my daddy deserved for somebody to write a book about his life, and now somebody has.

I wonder what this book will bring about. I have a feeling it will bring contact from a lot of other people who were somehow touched by my daddy. Please know, however, I am not responsible for any of his long-standing debts. Like Bob asked the man in Birmingham, how long did you know the Major before you allowed him into your wallet?

I may even get some answers from this book. There may be somebody out there who knows what demon got hold of Lewis McDonald Grizzard,

Sr., and will tell me. If that be the case, fine. There is no transgression for which I will not forgive him. None. As I said earlier, I have already thought the unthinkable.

There may be members of my family who think I have gone too far at times in this book. I apologize for anything they might think I should have not shared with the public. Any discomfort they may feel will be light in comparison to the pride I feel of having a book published about my daddy.

I can see clearly in retrospect the seed for the book was, indeed, first sown seventeen years ago on the day Daddy died. The frustrating emotions I felt then would become the main impetus for telling his story. I simply had to tell it. Life has its musts for all of us.

And then there was the night after tennis with my friend that is described in Chapter 1. "You ought to write a book about your daddy," he said. "It will make you feel better." It has.

A new character must be introduced here, and forgive me if at first she seems not to belong here. Believe me, she does.

Her name is Kathy. She was my third wife. Kathy has remarried since our divorce. She now lives in Montana with her two children and her new husband. I think they have some horses.

Kathy never knew my father, of course, but he would have liked her, and she would have adored the Major. What attracted me to Kathy in the first place was she laughed at my stories. She would have thought my daddy a riot.

Kathy saw the pattern so often. A few drinks, a

mention of my father, and then my tears. She never once scolded me for such displays.

She seemed to listen more closely than anybody else ever had when I talked about Daddy. She seemed genuinely interested.

We were at a dance several years ago. The band was playing oldies. The band began "The Tennessee Waltz." I asked Kathy to dance.

As we danced, I told her how this had been Mother's and Daddy's song.

> I was dancin'
> With my darlin'
> To the Tennessee Waltz
> When an old friend,
> I happened to see.
> I introduced him
> To my darlin'
> And while they were dancin'
> My friend stole my sweetheart away.

After the dance, Kathy said, "You ought to write a book about your daddy."

"I don't know if there is a book there," I said.

"There is a book," she went on, "and one day, you will write it."

As usual, Kathy was right. I am sending her one of the first copies of the book.

I wanted to mention my boyhood friend Ronnie Jenkins once more, too. Ronnie is married and he sells real estate now. I don't see him very often.

Ronnie went to the Dempsey and sobered up my daddy once when I couldn't go myself, and he went to his hip a couple of times for the Major, too. I think he admired Daddy's wanderlust. He once had a bit of it in himself.

Ronnie met Uncle John Wesley a few times, too, and he was taken by him as well. Ronnie used to laugh about Uncle John Wesley "messin' with a few ol' cars."

Ronnie was a comfort at Daddy's funeral. He even tried to convince my first wife to come back home. He didn't succeed, but at least he tried.

Ronnie had a nice thought at the funeral. "You know what it's going to be like in heaven when Uncle John Wesley dies and ties up with the Major? They'll be running the place in two weeks," he laughed.

I laughed, too.

"They'll wind up on a front porch somewhere with two rocking chairs. Every angel in the place will come just to listen to their stories. It'll take 'em ten thousand years before they'll have to start repeating themselves."

Uncle John Wesley died a few years back. He was up in his eighties and still smoking Camels.

I believe in heaven when I really want to. And when I think of Uncle John Wesley and my daddy rocking on a front porch in heaven with an admiring audience, I really want to.

I just hope heaven doesn't run out of Camels and fried chicken.

ABOUT THE AUTHOR

Lewis Grizzard was born in 1946 in Fort Benning, Georgia. He says he was raised poor, proud, and patriotic. His father—a military man—and his mother were divorced when he was six years old, after which he was raised mainly by his grandparents.

He graduated from the University of Georgia and at twenty-three became executive sports editor of the *Atlanta Journal.* He moved to the *Chicago Sun-Times* for a brief period as sports editor and then returned to Atlanta to become a columnist for the *Atlanta Constitution.* His column is now circulated to more than two hundred newspapers by King Features Syndicate.

He has written seven best-selling books, has been married and divorced three times, and now lives a single life with two dogs in a newly decorated home on the outskirts of Atlanta.